SUPERSELLERS

SUPERSELLERS

Portraits of Success from *Personal Selling Power*

Gerhard Gschwandtner
Laura B Gschwandtner

AMERICAN MANAGEMENT ASSOCIATION

This book is available at a special
discount when ordered in bulk quantities.
For information, contact Special Sales Department,
AMACOM, a division of American Management Association,
135 West 50th Street, New York, NY 10020.

Library of Congress Cataloging-in-Publication Data

Gschwandtner, Gerhard.
    Supersellers: portraits of success from Personal
selling power.

    1. Selling—Case studies.   2. Success in business—
United States—Case studies.   I. Gschwandtner, Laura B.
II. Personal selling power.   III. Title.
HF5438.25.G785   1986   658.8'5   86-47586
ISBN 0-8144-5883-1

Printing number

10 9 8 7 6 5 4 3 2 1

This book
is dedicated to
professional salespeople
who want to do better.

Acknowledgments

The 12 supersellers interviewed here have worked for more than 250 collective years to make this book possible. It is because of their determination, skill, drive, ambition, and creative energy that we have been able to produce this book at all. We thank them for their efforts.

The staff of *Personal Selling Power* has been of enormous help in keeping the home fires burning while we were out in the field. The loyalty and support of staff members are greatly appreciated.

The artists who lent their talents to this effort are to be congratulated for doing a superb job. For the drawings accompanying the Dr. Abraham Zaleznik and Pak Melwani interviews, Troy Howell used sensitivity and inventiveness. Ron Miller, who drew many of the portraits, called on a sensitive appreciation of the person behind each portrait in order to make these pages come alive. Scott Howson contributed to the finished manuscript with his elegant portrait of Steven McMillan, shown with the Electrolux mascot, and his portrait of IBM's F. G. "Buck" Rodgers.

The authors would like to thank Dr. Jack Schoenholtz for giving so freely of his time, his wisdom, and his extraordinary and intricate view of the world. It was through conversations with him that we were able to synthesize and clarify the issues surrounding the resolution of disappointment. He has acted as a guide, mentor, and enlightener. We would enter any tunnel with him confidently knowing he would help us find the light at the end.

Dr. Donald J. Moine, an organizational psychologist with the Association for Human Achievement in Redondo Beach, California, contributed the professional and perceptive analysis of Ed McMahon's boardwalk sales pitch for the Morris Metric Slicer. We thank him for his contribution.

Finally, to the backbone of our editorial efforts, our copy editor, Barbara Crookshanks, we extend special thanks for all she has done.

Gerhard Gschwandtner
L B Gschwandtner

A Note
on the Interviews

Some of the interviews in this book represent a joint effort by the authors. These include the interview with Dr. Abraham Zaleznik, which took place at Dr. Zaleznik's office at Harvard University's Graduate School of Business Administration; the interview with Ron Rice, which took place at the Hawaiian Tropic corporate headquarters in Daytona Beach, Florida; the interview with Mo Siegel, which took place at the Celestial Seasonings corporate headquarters in Boulder, Colorado; and the interview with Tony Schwartz, which took place at Mr. Schwartz's office/studio in New York City.

Of the remaining interviews, Gerhard Gschwandtner visited Ed McMahon in his dressing room at the NBC studios in Burbank, California; travelled to the corporate headquarters of Pilgrim Industries in Pittsburg, Texas, to interview Lonnie "Bo" Pilgrim; and attended the 1985 Direct Selling Association's annual meeting at The Homestead in Virginia's Bath County to interview Electrolux Chairman C. Steven McMillan. F. G. "Buck" Rodgers, former vice president of marketing for IBM Corporation, and Tom Hopkins, of Hopkins International, were both interviewed by Gerhard Gschwandtner over the telephone.

The interviews with Pak Melwani, founder and president of Royal Silk, Dr. Spencer Johnson, coauthor of *The One Minute Manager*, among other best-selling titles, and Barbara Proctor, of Proctor and Gardner Advertising, were done by L B Gschwandtner.

The interviews all originally appeared as features in *Personal Selling Power*.

Contents

SUPERSELLERS

Introduction

THE CRADLE OF AMBITION

The primary spring from which all the rivers of human achievement flow is ambition. It is never in short supply, but in an unharnessed form ambition can lead to frustration instead of accomplishment. In this book we have chosen to interview a select group of highly successful Americans whose ambitions have been harnessed into productive, goal-oriented achievements. They serve as shining examples of the positive flow that ambition can create when disappointments are met head on and resolved through work and self-awareness.

As we examine the life stories of the 12 successful individuals interviewed here—business leaders, entrepreneurs, motivators, a professor of business, even a famous entertainer and pitchman—the question of where their ambition came from takes on relevance for all of us. For in finding the source of that wellspring, we can identify the same fountain of ambition in our own lives as well. Once we see how ambition grows, we can begin to know our own, and to use it productively.

Just as success is a journey that has no end, so ambition is continually running through us. From the first awakening thoughts at daybreak to the last dreams of the night, ideas, fantasies, hopes, and plans all create the climate for ambition

1

The Disappointment Trap

to grow. The singular universal experience that initially allows ambition to take root, however, is disappointment. Without disappointment there would be no ambition. Without it, growth would lapse, development would languish, and we would all stand still: unmotivated, immovable, fixed—like boulders in the subsoil.

We all experience disappointments in life. Some are small: the personal disappointments of being passed over for a job, losing a sale, even growing older day by day. Other global disappointments can affect us deeply, as individuals or as a culture, and can have lasting repercussions. These disappointments, if we use them to grow and expand our view of ourselves and our world, often create a void—a void that forms the cradle of ambition.

No human being has ever achieved anything of significance without first having suffered a major disappointment, sometimes one that spans a period of many years. History is full of such examples. In this book, for instance, each of the 12 interview subjects had to fight through the battles of disappointment before arriving at a point where he or she had learned from and grown beyond them. In their struggle is a model for all of us to follow. No one can live our lives or weather our storms for us, but we can weather our own storms better by learning how other people weathered theirs, and when the winds blow and the rain beats against the door, we can remember the lessons from each of these supersellers, we can grow as they did, and we can achieve the results we want and deserve.

BEYOND DISAPPOINTMENT

Aside from birth, death, and sex, there is no other subject in human experience that is more universal than disappointment. Everyone has suffered disappointments, and everyone will suffer still more. Some people seem to have more than their fair share, while others linger over the feelings of the same disappointment, sometimes for years. Disappointment is truly a democratic experience. Citizens of every political and religious affiliation have experienced disappointments by the score. Rich and poor, educated and illiterate, Oriental and Occidental—all lives share this common thread.

Yet, to our knowledge, only one person has chosen to write on the subject of disappointment alone. Novels, biographies, short stories, and the like are rife with disappointment

A Postgraduate Course from the School of Hard Knocks

as shown through the lives of the characters. But it took one solitary thinker, a Harvard Business School professor, to delve into the subject and examine the drives and the potential for growth inherent in disappointment.

It is not news that we all survive disappointment. But it is news that we actually thrive because of it. How can that be? By what mechanism are we able to regroup and grow after a disappointment? That concern is at the heart of this book. This is not a philosophical look at the world through the eyes of intellectuals. Instead, this book shows how a dozen very practical people, whose core interest is to achieve success on many levels, have worked through their own disappointments and become rich in a variety of ways because of their un-daunted spirit and their ability to grow. It is a book about the practical aspects of the journey to greater achievement.

Unresolved disappointment leads inevitably to cynicism and a sense of defeat. Cynicism clouds the mind with thoughts that are designed to protect the self from further assault. Instead of protection, however, the thoughts shield the self from growth. Without growth, success—real success, the feeling that one has done a good and worthy job—is elusive.

In a world where disappointments are a daily occurrence, if one experiences only the disappointment, then no growth will occur. However, if we can pull the meaning out of the experience, if we can use it to measure our own self-esteem and define our own self-image, then we can promote independence and, through it, growth. Frustration and the disappointment associated with it are necessary to move ahead. A baby who never knows frustration will never get up and walk. If all its needs are met at all times, it will never want anything, and will never be able to get anything for itself. Such a person couldn't survive in adulthood. So we let our babies cry a little, and we allow them to feel angry at us when we don't fulfill their every wish immediately. They learn to gratify themselves in small ways, and they grow up and finally stand on their own.

As adults, we are no different. If we always see the world from our own eye-level, we miss the opportunity just above and beyond our vision. When the emotions are touched by disappointment, the brain is programmed to react. In the reaction are the currents that bring new ideas to life. And new ideas are what makes ambition grow in positive ways. Old ideas tend to fester like sores. They can make us sickly and can cause pain—and they do not allow for growth. Without growth, disappointment lingers. And, most ironically, disappointment, when resolved, is the stuff from which real success will grow. The disappointments we suffer today will be with us, in one form or another, for the rest of our lives. It is what we choose to do with them that is significant and that has real impact on the quality of our lives and the quantity of our riches.

1

The Management of Disappointment

Dr. Abraham Zaleznik

"I believe that both the great strengths and weaknesses of gifted leaders often hinge on how they manage disappointment."

Early in 1982, I went to the Library of Congress in Washington, D.C., to research the subject of success. I found over 1,200 books under that category: In addition there were 220 titles on the subject of winning with only 16 on losing. I began to wonder whether failure was indeed the natural opposite of success, and concluded that, when success was absent, disappointment was the more common state. I hurried back to the Library's computer and card files to look for all the titles in the Library of Congress—in three languages, English, German, and French—under the subject heading "disappointment."

I reasoned that, disappointment being probably the most common human emotion after love, I could anticipate a good month's work to sift through all the published material. It thus came as an enormous surprise when not one single title appeared. Instead there was only one magazine article, "The Management of Disappointment," by Dr. Abraham Zaleznik (*The Harvard Business Review*, Nov.–Dec. 1967, pp. 59–70).

Two years and much work later, Laura B Gschwandtner, (who is editor-in-chief of *Personal Selling Power* as well as my wife) and I made a pilgrimage of sorts to Cambridge, Massachusetts, and the office of Dr. Zaleznik at Harvard University's School of Business Administration. It was a cool fall day, the leaves were just beginning to turn, and that day Dr. Zaleznik inspired two more years of work that culminated in this book. During that time, Dr. Zaleznik has been written about in publications like *The New York Times* and *The Wall Street Journal*. He has become well known as a sort of post-psychoanalytic management guru.

Our experience with him was of a more personal nature. We went to talk about how the management of disappointment can affect a career. "In the 16 years since I first published that article," he told us, "you are the first people who have showed any interest at all in the subject." "Why was that?" we asked. "Because people see disappointment as a down and they don't want to be associated with anything that is not up and positive. Furthermore," he went on, "once exposed, people don't know what to do with these feelings and that frightens them."

All the more reason to write about the subject of disappointment, we decided. We were told by numerous people that we were making a mistake and that our readers would not respond favorably to any subject that was not positive in nature. But we felt that people are interested in what drives them. They want to know what will help them to achieve more, and they want to understand how they can improve their lives.

Our instincts proved to be right when the January/February 1984 issue of *Personal Selling Power*, with Dr. Zaleznik's disappointment trap featured prominently on the cover, sold more copies than any previous issue, and continued to break sales records for *Personal Selling Power* for a year and a half after its initial publication.

During the interview, Dr. Zaleznik was gracious, intelligent, and provocative. The groundwork he laid has been a great boon to many readers, and stands as a pioneering work for all the interviews contained in this book. After reading his thoughts on the management of disappointment, we find it easy to see how the careers of the supersellers in this book reached such pinnacles of achievement. Zaleznik is a rare bird in the management flock. He dwells on the person not the task. He talks of the feelings, not the bottom line. He teaches the insights that will lead to deeper meaning and higher success.

It is easy to forget that business people are *people* first, and *business people* second. Those who operate from a base of unresolved disappointment are likely to become mediocre managers at best. Those who rank their business successes second to their feelings of self-worth are likely to have little of the former. A person who follows a path of growth after a disappointment will be a stable force on the team. Dr. Abraham Zaleznik's humanization of business is serving us well now and, we predict, will go on to serve our needs for growth in the future.

In re-reading the interview with Dr. Zaleznik more than two years after its initial publication, we still find much indepth and thought-provoking material. In his own environment at one of the world's most revered institutions of higher learning, Harvard University, Zaleznik is a favorite of the students and a rare commodity on the management scene. This interview with him attests to the fact that one independent thinker can account for enough ripples on a pond to start a tidal wave of sorts. Riding this wave can bring the reader to new shores, richer fields, and more fertile valleys.

Dr. Abraham Zaleznik, the son of a Philadelphia produce market owner, has studied the inner workings of the business world as a director of five companies, including the Ogden Corporation, Purity Supreme, and Pueblo International.

Dr. Zaleznik, who holds a doctorate in commercial science, approaches the subject of disappointment from a unique vantage point. He is, in fact, a certified clinical psychoanalyst, one of the few who make psychoanalytic thought and concepts accessible to business leaders and managers.

He teaches at the Boston Psychoanalytic Society and at Harvard University Graduate School of Business Administration. Early last year, Harvard University appointed Dr. Zaleznik the Konosuke Matsushita Professor of Leadership. From 1967-1983 he was the Cahners-Rabb Professor of Social Psychology of Management, Harvard Business School.

"Disappointment becomes a particularly significant experience,"explains Dr. Zaleznik, referring to business executives, "because people don't know what to do." During the interview he referred to the suicide of Alan David Saxon, the Los Angeles gold dealer whose death touched off a search for $60 million in precious metals presumed missing. His tone of voice revealed his concern for the tragic loss.

His concern for the individual in an organization is reflected in his penetrating books (Power and the Corporate Mind, Houghton Mifflin, 1975; Orientation and Conflict in Career, Harvard, 1975; Human Dilemmas of Leadership, Harper & Row, 1966) and many articles (see Harvard Business Review: "Managers and Leaders," May/June 1977, and "Management of Disapointment," Nov./Dec. 1967).

We met with Dr. Zaleznik in his Harvard University office, which is not only equipped with the proverbial psychoanalyst's couch, but also with a modern computer which is linked to the one at his home and another at his Florida "hideaway." This linkage suggests that he practices what he preaches as a first line defense against disappointment: "Don't put all your eggs in one basket."

PSP: *Dr. Zaleznik, you are a pioneer in researching the subject of disappointment. What does disappointment mean?*

Zaleznik: Let's start with a superficial definition. You want something, you don't get it, the result is disappointment. But disappointment is not simply the result of not getting what one wants or expects. We need to examine what it is about that want that grabs a psychological bite. What a person wants often has enormous unconscious value and, consequently, not getting it takes on a great deal of significance. The psychological event of disappointment may lead the individual to fall back on himself and discover that the world and his place in it has no meaning. One tragic example that made headlines [in 1984] is the gold dealer in Los Angeles who killed himself. There has been a whole rash of suicides. . . .

PSP: *So you are saying that not getting what we want is not necessarily the key issue, it's the unconscious meaning we attach to these wants that creates the disappointment. . . .*

Zaleznik: Right. Let's say a person charges a business venture with certain unrealistic dreams. Not getting what he wants can lead to disappointment, and so can getting what he wants. When a person finally gets what he has been working so hard for and sees that his unconscious dreams aren't realized, the result will be a tremendous disappointment. Take Henry Ford; his achievement of the Model T marked a turning point in his career. He became inceasingly rigid and unrealistic in his thinking, he seemed to have experienced some disappointment in a fantasy attached to his achievement.

PSP: *What are the most common misconceptions people have about disappointment?*

Zaleznik: One, that it is bad. Two, . . . that if we are disappointed, we are not supposed to show it.

PSP: *Denial is encouraged.*

Zaleznik: Yes, it is. If people show and react to their disappointment in public, they are going to hurt themselves. In a sense they are trapped if they don't know how to get help. Business is preoccupied with success. The world loves a winner, nobody likes a loser. So, people expect that they have to come on with the bright, cheerful, upbeat mask, because the world loves a winner. That's where I say it takes a great deal of courage. You have to be able to think, to experience what's going on, but at the same time recognize that nobody has a lot of sympathy.

PSP: *So disappointment should not be viewed as negative and it isn't equal to failure.*

Zaleznik: No, it doesn't equal failure. Once it is seen in positive terms, I think people are then prepared to learn a great deal from the experience.

PSP: *Do you think that the positive thinker prevents, avoids, or denies disappointment?*

Zaleznik: There are various types of positive thinkers. There are some who have deep faith—like Dr. Norman Vincent Peale. I don't know him personally, but I believe that he views that God has put him here to do something. That is a powerful belief that can sustain a person for a long time. He has a mission to accomplish in life and there is no such thing as disappointment in the sense that the mission doesn't go away. Therefore, if you're lost, it simply means you haven't gotten there yet.

PSP: *You said that there are different types of positive thinkers.*

Zaleznik: There are some positive thinkers who "think positive" because it pays. There is a market for it. They have good marketing sense. They appeal to a wide range of fantasies. Positive thinking is part of the national character. If you don't like your job, you leave it and go elsewhere; if things don't work out there, you go someplace else.

PSP: *It is part of the American Dream.*
Zaleznik: There are also those in the field of self-improvement, who say that if you change the way you think about life and situations, it's going to get better and everything will work well.
PSP: *Is that realistic?*
Zaleznik: It serves as a valuable myth for people who believe it. But it may not necessarily lead people to deal with the realities of whatever they are good at. The criticism I would have of certain positive thinkers is that they don't always understand that people have to develop disciplines and talents. Some are even holding out a false promise that it's easy: If I believe hard enough, I could become it. What nonsense! My friends in Austria have a word they use quite a lot: *Blödsinn*. What does that mean?
PSP: *Idiocy.*
Zaleznik: It's used a lot in Vienna.
PSP: *Are you saying that a positive thinker should spend more energy in developing the talents necessary to achieve?*
Zaleznik: Let's look at this issue from a different angle. I think the most tragic positive thinker of all time was Arthur Miller's Willy Loman in "The Death of a Salesman." His character was a beautiful illustration of the idea that if you spend so much time attached to the dream and no time figuring out what it is that you are capable of doing, you are bound to get disappointed. Instead of improving your talents, you are living with an illusion. That's my objection to positive thinkers. In life you need courage, but you don't need illusion.
PSP: *How would you define courage?*
Zaleznik: Courage is the willingness to look at life as it is, to look at yourself as you are, and to come to terms.
PSP: *So you are saying it takes more courage to look at life as it is than to think positive?*
Zaleznik: Yes, because you don't need a screen to look at reality.
PSP: *What are the most common reactions to disappointment? Are there certain stages people go through?*

Zaleznik: Many people get depressed, which is not entirely bad. There is also a pre-depressive reaction, a manic episode, in which people become hyperactive. It's a very dangerous time when they make rotten decisions and usually get themselves into trouble. They are better off getting depressed. To understand the true nature of depression you have to understand rage. I won't say anger, because when there is a quantitative effect, it becomes rage. If you want to talk in terms of stages of disappointment, we would simply be looking at the transformations of rage.

PSP: *Rage directed at . . . ?*

Zaleznik: Rage toward oneself for falling short. The enormous shame or humiliation that one has not measured up to the ego ideal [*image of the ideal self*]. Rage directed at others who didn't fulfill, rage at those who are withholding. I think that with all the openness in this society about sexuality, the big ugly secret is about rage. In this sense, disappointment becomes a particularly significant experience, because people don't know what to do. They are not familiar with the experience of anger, or rage. They don't know how to simulate it and deal with it. In our society the emphasis is on teamwork, on getting along. So there is little room for dealing with disappointment.

PSP: *How can we deal with it?*

Zaleznik: You can begin by accepting a kind of passive moment in connection with the disappointment. Withdraw from the battle. I don't mean to give up your job or family, but make a kind of psychological retreat. Allow yourself to deal with the experience. There are two ways people react to psychological difficulties: One kind of person tends to interact with others, the other kind begins to think. I think that the latter person has more going for him in the long run.

PSP: *You are talking about introspection and self-examination. I would guess that this is not the typical, everyday way of dealing with disappointment.*

Zaleznik: No, it is not, because there are certain social pressures. People can't withdraw very well. But again, this is a very creative thing to know how to do. You have to have good fall-back positions in which you're using your talents to reacquaint yourself or to discover something new. Many great leaders have worked through their disappointments and emerged with greater strength. For example, Winston Churchill suffered great disappointment during World War I. He learned how to paint, he wrote and refocussed his energies from the outer world to himself.

PSP: *Do you see a way to prevent or reduce the risk of suffering disappointment?*

Zaleznik: One sign of wisdom and maturity is to piece out one's ego investments. Unfortunately, very talented people often don't know how to piece things out and suffer catastrophic disappointment because they have put all their eggs in one basket.

PSP: *How about professional salespeople. How can they minimize the risks of suffering disappointment?*

Zaleznik: It's an interesting issue, because selling takes a curious combination of desire and motivation, but it also takes a very realistic understanding of what you are selling, to whom, and for what purpose. You have to get that in a proper balance or one characteristic drives out the other. One of the things that I judge to be very important is not to mistake success and failure as being loved and not loved. If salespeople personalize selling in these terms, then their self-esteem is on the line. They set themselves up for disappointment. If I were in selling, I would try to get that under control.

PSP: *What would you consider a good preventive measure?*

Zaleznik: I would develop expert knowledge about the product, the customer, the market, and the competition. I would look at these facts realistically, examine the pluses and minuses, and then be prepared to sell under those terms. I would not think of the sale just as the product of a winning personality. On the other hand, I realize that you have to have a lot of motivation to go out and sell.

PSP: *How would you deal with a customer's disappointment?*

Zaleznik: Isn't this what makes a top salesperson? I would try to sort out what the prospect expects from the product and deal with that prior to the sale. Customers know that there are certain limitations and need to understand what they are paying for. I think a good salesperson tries to do a very good job examining what a prospect needs to accomplish with the product. Also, experience will tell you what people are looking for and what illusions they bring with them. Effective selling takes a very good sense of how the world works. It also takes self-knowledge.

PSP: *Where would you put the emphasis?*

Zaleznik: On both.

PSP: *This requires a lot of thinking. . . .*

Zaleznik: Yes. One of the greatest virtues of the human mind is that you can think in relatively inexpensive terms. Action is always very expensive. Why not get the maximum mileage out of experience by thinking about it and doing less? The beauty of the human mind is that thinking is an experimental form of action—very inexpensive. There is no charge for thinking.

PSP: *You've talked about Winston Churchill. How do you see General Patton and how he handled disappointment?*

Zaleznik: Based on what I have read in biographies, I believe he never really came to terms with his fear about lack of manliness and courage. He became a superb field general reactively, because he was afraid of himself. One book documented that under moments of great stress and battlefield activity, he would take his pulse and he would find it had accelerated and would be self-condemnatory. He was too hard on himself, but he also had difficulty understanding the nature of his fears. In that sense, he was vulnerable and susceptible to taking a lot of risks. As a commander, you have to remember that you must take care of your subordinates; otherwise, they will lose hope. The hope they have is that their authority figures have their best interests at heart and if they are sent on a dangerous mission, it's for the good of all. They don't do it to harm you. Commanders are calculating what is in the best interest of everybody.

PSP: *How about your own disappointments. What was your biggest disappointment?*

Zaleznik: When my father died, I was 20 years old and never had the chance to do with him what every young man wishes he could do with his father, which is to be close and to look at the world through his eyes for a while. That was the gravest of all disappointments for me. I got over it, but it took a very long time. That was a terrible experience.

PSP: *You once wrote that preoccupation with success may be less important than the role of disappointment in the evolution of a career.*

Zaleznik: Yes. I believe that both the great strengths and weaknesses of gifted leaders often hinge on how they manage disappointments, which are inevitable in life. There are a number of studies and psychological biographies that support this conclusion.

PSP: *Could you give us a few examples?*

Zaleznik: One would be Erik Erickson's psychological biography of Gandhi or John Mack's study of Lawrence of Arabia. There are excellent works analyzing leaders like Henry Ford, Frederick Taylor, John Stuart Mill, and many more.

PSP: *Based on these studies and your own experience, do you see disappointment as a growth factor?*

Zaleznik: Yes.

PSP: *Would you say that if you haven't had any disappointment, you haven't had any growth?*

Zaleznik: I would say that.

PSP: *In which areas do you feel women manage disappointment better or worse than men?*

Zaleznik: I think that they are more vulnerable by the social pressures that restrict them from showing how they feel about things. In business, if your heart is on your sleeve, you're going to get hurt badly. I would think of this as a cultural problem. It's harder for them.

PSP: *How do you separate your heart from your sleeve?*

Zaleznik: By cultivating a sense of separateness, by seeing one's self in terms of being different. I don't mean being isolated, but being separate.

PSP: *Separating the task from the person.*

Zaleznik: Yes, and getting a very clear understanding about what is going on within oneself in the situation, so one's emotion can be dealt with.

PSP: *How about the role of drive and ambition in disappointment?*

Zaleznik: I think you could make an analogy with golf. The more ambitious you are, the more difficulties you may experience with the game. Perhaps the most effective people are those who modify ambition. Ambition is different from drive. Drive is the desire for mastery, competence, ability, and honing one's talents. Ambition is essentially a blind impulse. Instead of trying to work at what you are doing and to be better at it, one projects a lot of energy toward vague goals.

PSP: *Where does the healthy drive end and burning ambition begin?*

Zaleznik: The healthy drive ends when you can't tolerate waiting. Burning ambition is filled with impatience. One is torn and restless. But for some people, it's just a fact of life. I wouldn't try to change them, that's the way they are. We always have to keep in mind that there is a powerful engine in the human being that can lead to great achievement. People often ask if it's analyzed, what will happen. My response to that is, nothing will happen, if there is real talent there.

PSP: *Let's assume that a person has real talent and works himself to the top. Let's also assume that that person has no unrealistic dreams connected to his goals. Do you feel that this talented and ambitious person will be lonely at the top?*

Zaleznik: This is a myth. It's not lonely at the top. Henry Kissinger once said that power is the greatest aphrodisiac. I would say that power can be very therapeutic and I think that people at the top have the greatest life. Don't feel sorry for them. Of course, there is envy, but that's very small compared to the riches one can enjoy in a position of accomplishment.

... but how are you going to deal with your next disappointment?

Disappointment—What's in It for Me?

*"In our society the emphasis is on teamwork, on getting along. So there is
little room for dealing with disappointment."*
                                                    —Dr. Abraham Zaleznik

What were your biggest disappointments this year? What
expectations or dreams did not get fulfilled? Think of a few
more. You are now ready to figure your D/G ratio.

D/G stands for Disappointment versus Growth. (Remember, disappointment comes first, growth second.) Here is how
it works: Begin by listing your ten major disappointments
from last year on a sheet of paper. Then count the number of
unresolved disappointments. (The ones that still have a bitter
taste as you think about them.) Next, count the number of
disappointments that have increased your strengths. Let's say
that you still have negative feelings about that one large order
that you didn't get (but felt so sure about) and that you had to
fire one salesperson (with whom you had spent so much
time—but he still didn't improve).

Let's also assume that you've managed all other disappointments well, so your D/G ratio would be 2/8. The first
figure indicates that you have two disappointment-manage-
ment opportunities left for next year. The second figure indicates your growth capacity. Since you managed 8 out of 10
disappointments, your present growth capacity is 80 percent.
If you add another unresolved disappointment in the first
quarter of next year, your growth capacity would then drop to
70 percent. What does this mean to your chances of reaching
your goals for next year?

Simple. To the extent that you deny (unresolved) disappointments, you will deprive yourself of potential growth. On
the other hand, every time you manage your disappointments
well, you'll increase your growth potential.

Our interview with Dr. Zaleznik clearly demonstrates that disappointments don't equal failure; they are instead opportunities for growth. "Preoccupation with success may be less important than the role of disappointment in the evolution of a career," asserts Dr. Zaleznik. He refers to a number of psychological biographies of gifted leaders to support the idea that the way we manage disappointment may ultimately become responsible for our achieving success.

That's reason enough to use disappointments as stepping stones. Disappointment is nothing but an opportunity in disguise.

Working Your Way
Out of the Disappointment Trap

by Dr. Jack Schoenholtz

Two Kinds of Hurt

Disappointment can be separated into two major categories: global disappointments (the serious kind) and everyday disappointments.

A global disappointment has a tendency to become pathological. When people get depressed following a severe disappointment, they tend to become incapable of reexamining the conflicts and issues that have preceded the disappointment. They may produce certain chemicals in the brain that prevent them from looking (optimistically) with clear eyes at anything. In these instances, professional help (from a psychiatrist, psychologist, or mental health center) is essential.

Everyday disappointments are challenges for self-management and opportunities for personal growth. The everyday disappointment is the counterpart of the gratification–frustration experience, necessary for development from childhood on.

Are you suffering from a minor disappointment? Congratulate yourself. It only means that you're growing. Constant gratification would be like living in a 100 percent sterile environment—totally unrealistic.

Establish New Priorities

Stop running. Think. Review your experience. If you are alone, put it on paper. If you have access to a good friend, talk it over. If the disappointment is related to your job, discuss it with your spouse first. Isolate minor disappointments before you see your next customer!

Minimize Your Exposure

One major source of disappointment is unrealistic expectations. We often over-estimate what our abilities can do, what money can do, what authority can do, what contracts can do, and what other people will do for us. Disappointment in expectations helps us learn about the practical opportunities in life. Unrealistic self-expectations can lead to unnecessary disappointments. For example, Omar Bradley always considered himself a soldier; George Patton always considered himself a general. Patton could not live with anything less than total command of the situation, whereas Bradley served his Commander-in-Chief.

Action Tip: Know what you expect and why. Assign probabilities to your expectations. Example: One close in five calls = 100%. Close in one call = 20%.

Increase Your Resistance

One key way to lower your chances for suffering disappointment is to increase your ability to tolerate love and hate and avoid confusing them with indifference. How? Through commitment. Why? If your commitment to your job, your mission, or your goal is the global reason for deploying your energies, then love or hate do not become the personal reasons for doing something. For example: A deep commitment to customer satisfaction allows you to accept love and hate. In selling, some prospects will accept you and some will reject you; some will just be indifferent. Your commitment will help you tolerate the different feelings that prospects have about you and the situation. It will help you understand that a rejection may be real or imagined. It may just be indifference, nothing but a reflection of their world and the particular situation.

Your deep commitment doesn't change the direction of your drives; it will help you move beyond love and hate. Commitments can transform the roadblocks of love and hate into clear pathways.

Put the Odds in Your Favor

Don't put all your eggs in one basket. Monitor your expectations. Know your abilities and their limits. Increase your tolerance for love and hate. Keep your eyes open to your dreams. Renew your commitments every day. Learn to accept other people's negative feelings. Accept your vulnerability. Maintain conscious control over your drives. Build close relationships. Keep reaching higher than you expect. Get professional help when the hurt is alarmingly deep or someone close to you notices. Think.

Bottom Line: Accept disappointments as growth experiences. Learn from them, or you'll sidestep growth by becoming cynical. Cynicism is the scar tissue of unresolved disappointment.

Dr. Jack G. Schoenholtz is Medical Director of Rye Psychiatric Hospital Center, Rye, N.Y., and Clinical Associate Professor of Psychiatry, New York Medical College.

2

The Top Banana

Ed McMahon

"All the good techniques of performing and acting are used in selling."

Ed McMahon—salesman, pitchman, actor, director, producer, announcer, TV show host, straight man, comic, professional product endorser (the list seems endless)—has become
one of the most successful show business personalities this
country has ever produced. At any one time he is likely to
have at least three network TV shows running concurrently,
with his well-known face appearing for scores of companies'
products on local and national commercials. It is reputed that
his income is well above that of his famous boss, "Tonight
Show" host Johnny Carson.

This giant of stage and screen has an unequaled love for
selling. Beginning as a kid selling newspapers and lemonade,
he later made history on the boardwalk in Atlantic City, New
Jersey, pitching the Morris Metric Slicer to passersby. His
wonderful autobiography, *Here's Ed* (New York: G. P. Putnam's Sons, 1976), testifies to his incredible ability to create
opportunities where others see only problems.

When we decided to contact him for an interview, it was
with little hope that it would be granted. But, surprisingly, his
assistant Madeline Kelly told us in her clipped British accent,
"Oh, I'm sure Ed would love to do that. He's always considered himself a salesman." Ed graciously consented and I
showed up with my tape recorder at his dressing room in—
yes, folks—downtown Burbank and was ushered in to find a
typical Hollywood scene.

McMahon was seated in a reclining chair with a mono-
grammed towel draped over a bare foot while a manicurist
plied her trade with dedication and professionalism. He
waved a hearty, "Come in, come in," beckoning me to a chair
nearby. We began to talk—about the past, his incredible experiences as a Marine pilot, the early days as a bingo show
announcer, and his idol, W. C. Fields. Ed is a remarkable story-
teller, and whether he talks about commercials, selling, success, food, or his non-stop schedule, he doesn't do it to
impress you, but to share his boundless excitement about
doing the best job he possibly can.

Anyone who still thinks of Ed McMahon as Johnny Carson's announcer and straight man had better take a closer look. This man is a total professional whose work schedule puts the average workaholic to shame. Taping over 600 commercials a year, sometimes an astounding eight on a single day, McMahon goes regularly to the office for a full day's producing schedule or to the studio to tape a series of TV shows. He never stops, and seems never to falter. In the precarious world of show business, Ed McMahon can always be counted on for a thoroughly professional performance on the first take.

During the interview, he was open and upbeat, talking about every subject under the sun with enthusiasm. He is a man who loves life and relishes his place in it. A polished performer and lover of fine food, Ed is also a sartorial dresser. Once he puts on his suit to do his thing on "The Tonight Show," he doesn't sit down until it's time to take his place on the couch next to Johnny. Why? Because sitting would wrinkle his suit, and Ed, ever the perfectionist, wants to feel perfect, look perfect, and give the best performance his heart knows he can give when he steps in front of the cameras and millions of TV viewers. Ed recently got his star on the Hollywood Walk of Fame—it's right next to the star of his idol, W. C. Fields.

In the entertainment world, what goes on behind the scenes is more complex and much more difficult than the easy-as-pie scenes the audience sees played out. McMahon lives with pressure. And he thrives on it. His approach to his work, in all its variety and complexity, is that of the honeybee darting from flower to flower, working with efficiency and speed, collecting just what's necessary to produce the honey that will feed the entire hive.

McMahon has been feeding the public for decades, ever since he hawked his first bingo show from the back of a truck. His work has meaning because it makes us look at ourselves and smile. His salesmanship has established professional standards that we would all do well to emulate—he's a man who helps us all set a wish on fire.

On May 18, 1984, Ed McMahon received the Horatio Alger Award, a distinctive honor given to people who have come from humble backgrounds and have made extraordinary achievements. Ed McMahon is a superachiever. Although he is nationally recognized as one of TV's biggest stars ("The Tonight Show," "Star Search," and "TV Bloopers"), only a few people know about his outstanding abilities and skills in selling.

He discovered his selling talents at a very early age. Upon hearing that he could earn a bicycle by selling subscriptions to the Saturday Evening Post, *he sold three the same afternoon. (He rode his own bike shortly thereafter). As a speech and drama student at Catholic University in Washington D.C., he supported his wife and child by selling stainless steel cookware door to door.*

During the summer he perfected his techniques by pitching products on the boardwalk in Atlantic City. His talents as a master salesman and master showman are two powerful drives that have advanced his career far beyond his own dreams.

Personal Selling Power was privileged to spend an unforgettable afternoon with Ed in his Burbank office. Here is the eye-opening transcript of our discussion.

PSP: *In a recent interview with the* **Los Angeles Times,** *you said, "I am proud to be a salesman." What is it about selling that makes you proud?*

McMahon: Well, it's an ability, like the ability to play the trumpet, or to tap dance. It's a great asset to have. I was very lucky to discover at a very young age that I could sell. As a kid, I used to sell the *Bayonne Times.* I bought the papers for a penny and sold them for two pennies.

PSP: *You were in business for yourself?*

McMahon: Yes, if I didn't sell those newspapers, I had to eat my profits. We used to customize our pitch according to the neighborhood. In a poor neighborhood we would holler about the new relief programs. In a rich neighborhood, we'd pitch the latest news about the stock market. I used to sell out every day.

PSP: *Do you feel that salespeople in general are not proud of their profession?*

McMahon: Well, some say, "I'm just a salesman," and don't have the pride they should have. Several years ago, I read about a researcher who interviewed people about their work. He found that the majority didn't like their jobs. This was surprising to me because I love my work and can't wait to get started in the morning. I love it when someone is enthusiastic about what they are doing.

PSP: *In your autobiography,* **Here's Ed,** *you mention, "I have the mind and instincts of a hustler." What did you mean by that?*

McMahon: I used the word hustler to describe someone who would take almost nothing and make something out of it. As a kid, one of the first things I ever did was sell pineapple juice. I didn't have a lemonade stand; I wanted to do things differently. I loaded the stand with pineapples. My uncle used to tease me by saying, "He loses 2¢ on every glass he sells, but the volume eats up the loss." *[He laughs heartily—that famous McMahon belly laugh.]* By hustling, I mean the ability to start something from scratch and get something going—which I have done many times in my life.

PSP: *How would you describe your qualities as a salesman?*

McMahon: One of the things I learned very early is to use positive statements in selling. The choice of words is very important. When I was selling pots and pans, the question of price would always come up. When the prospect would ask, "How much does it cost?" my answer would be, "That depends on how you are going to purchase it." The next quality would be the use of positive body language. For instance, I sold fountain pens on the boardwalk in Atlantic City. I learned that you don't pick up a fountain pen like just anybody else does, you pick it up like this. *[He carefully lifts up an imaginary pen.]* You see, the way you handle it . . . is like a piece of jewelry. Your body language says: This is special, this is a fine writing instrument, this is better than somebody else's.

PSP: *Did your stage experience help you in selling?*

McMahon: Of course. All the good techniques of performing and acting are used in selling. Also, I learned to limit the choices. One time I set up a counter for a dealer who offered many different colored fountain pens. I told him, "I want red and green. Don't give me any other colors." He couldn't understand that, but I wanted to limit the choices. In my pitch, there was a point where I asked the customer, "If you were to buy this pen, would you prefer the red one or the green one?" So they've got to make a choice. Let's say the customer answered, "Red is my favorite color." I'd say, "I am awfully fond of red myself. Let me just put this red pen in your hand. Would you write with it and see how it feels?" Eliminating choices is very important. You don't offer 20 things to sell, just a couple.

PSP: *You mentioned acting and selling. How do you see the similarities between the qualities of a salesman and the qualities of a showman?*

McMahon: Selling and showmanship have one element in common that is so vital for success: First, you have to have their attention. No matter whether your audience consists of a single person or 100,000 people, before you can sell or show them anything, you have to get their focus on you.

PSP: *How?*

McMahon: As a showman, the first thing you have to do is to get your audience together into one unit. Like when I come out to do the warm-up for "The Tonight Show": Here are people from all walks of life, different social backgrounds, financial backgrounds, and ethnic backgrounds. My job is to get them all together as a unit. It's like making a necklace, where you take a lot of pearls and put them on a string. When I am finished with the warm-up, I turn that necklace over to Johnny Carson.

PSP: *That's a nice analogy.*

McMahon: Sometimes, when you're emceeing a show, you can get a noisy crowd . . . especially people who have paid a lot of money for their seats. They are important—at least they think they are important. They are important in their professions, in society. They are a little blasé, they are drinking, talking to each other, and you want them to listen to you.

PSP: *How?*

McMahon: I have a great device! I will finally intimidate them if I have to go that far. I'll say, "Friends, I agreed to come here tonight, I've got no place to go, it's the only place I'm going to go to tonight. Nothing is going to happen back there—everything is going to happen right here. Everything that's important to this show is going to come from right here. So whenever you're ready, you'll let me know by your silence." And then I wait. I just wait until they finally realize that nothing is happening. As they quiet down, I continue, "Now that I've got all your attention, we've got a wonderful show for you tonight. . . ." I don't have to do that now, but in the early days, before they knew who I was, I had to do this with tougher crowds.

PSP: *Have you ever used this in selling?*

McMahon: It's the same. When I was peddling pots and pans in someone's house and the kids were running back and forth, I would say something like, "Perhaps I might come back at another time. . . ." And they would respond, "No, no, no. . . . Jimmy and Mary, go to your room. . . ." You see, when the kids are distracting, I wouldn't have their attention and I couldn't make the sale.

PSP: *You need to set the stage for your presentation.*

McMahon: Yes, exactly.

PSP: *You have an interesting way of choosing words and telling stories. Where did you learn that?*

McMahon: My father was a great story-teller. I learned by listening to him. He would take an ordinary story and embellish it. I remember when he and his cronies would come back from a fishing trip and someone would start to tell a story about something that happened, they would always stop and say, "Let Eddy tell it," because it would be a better story, it would have more elements, he embellished it. That's one of the great gifts I got from him. I still use that.

PSP: *A good story can be a very persuasive tool if it's told well.*

McMahon: There is nothing more annoying than hearing someone tell a story during a dinner party, "I heard this great story," and halfway through he tells you, "Oh, I forgot to tell you, the guy is a priest." By then, you don't want to hear more. If you want to tell a good story, you begin by setting the scene, like: *[He lowers his voice.]* "There was this priest in a tiny little village . . ." You have to set up the story, you need to have an objective, a direction.

PSP: *When you were selling on the boardwalk in Atlantic City, you pitched the Morris Metric Vegetable Slicer.*

McMahon: The famous Morris Metric Slicer. Yes. I was a pitchman, and they are a very exclusive group of people. It was a well-paying job: I made $500 a week on the boardwalk in the late 1940s.

PSP: *How long did it take you to learn that pitch?*

McMahon: Not long at all. I just hung around, watched the Morris brothers do it and took the best parts of all. I finally convinced them to let me try to sell the Morris Metric Slicer at 8:00 in the morning. It was the worst time of the day to be selling on the boardwalk. But people stopped and listened and bought. Soon, I would match what the salesman was producing at 10 A.M. As I got better, they would give me the choice hours. I became one of the top salesmen in the business.

PSP: *What was your first job as a showman?*

McMahon: My first paid job was in the back of a sound truck, announcing that a big fair was going to take place. I made up my own spiel, I made up jokes, and I was successful. Then I got a job announcing a horse-racing game at a resort.

PSP: *This led you to the bingo business?*

McMahon: Yes. I got the bingo job. That was a big job. I was not only the announcer, but I became the manager and also drove the semi-trailer with all the bingo equipment.

PSP: *That was right after you finished high school.*

McMahon: Yes, I was just a kid. But that's how I made a living.

PSP: *You said once, "You can sell almost anything if you go about it the right way and work hard enough." Do you think that a lot of people know the right way, but don't work hard enough?*

McMahon: Sure.

PSP: *What seems to be the reason?*

McMahon: I think it's the inability to handle rejection. When I sold pots and pans from door to door, I worked every night from 6:00 to 10:00 in the evening. Sometimes at 9:00 I hadn't sold anything, but I was still out on the road making calls. One evening at 9:45, I sold three sets. I dropped in on a family, they were having friends over, and everyone bought. If I had quit at 9:15, I wouldn't have sold anything that night. I persevered and I kept trying.

PSP: *How do you suggest salespeople deal with rejection?*

McMahon: First of all, you are not unique when you get rejected. Being rejected is not something that you've invented, it doesn't just happen to you alone. When I first went to New York, I won the first audition. I figured that I've got this place in my pocket, but I lost the next 30 jobs. That got me straightened out quickly. In selling, you know that you're going to be rejected or turned down, that's the nature of the beast. It's a built-in part, it comes with the territory. You can't be a salesperson without failing. I guess everybody can find their own way of overcoming it. For me, it was perseverance, pressing on, discipline. It's knowing that sooner or later you get back on track.

PSP: *What was the worst rejection you've ever experienced?*

McMahon: I got a chance to become the announcer on a comedy game show in New York. I did what I thought was a great warm-up and did everything right. The following week I did the same show and I assumed that everything was fine and wonderful, but they fired me. Nobody would tell me why. I got on the train home to Philadelphia and figured my career was over and I'd better get out of show business and back to selling. Later on, I found out that I got fired because the producer took exception to a joke I told. That was the worst rejection for me. But interestingly, after a few years went by, I auditioned for a new TV show. The same producer who fired me liked me so well, he wanted me to host two of his shows. Since NBC didn't want to let the same person host two shows, I ended up doing only one.

PSP: *Which one?*

McMahon: "Snap Judgment."

PSP: *Great. How important is humor in selling?*

McMahon: I think it is very important for two reasons. First, it's a great tool for breaking the ice and for eliminating buying reluctance. Second, it makes the presentation less boring for me. I stay more in focus and more interested if I'm going to do a joke and get a laugh. On the boardwalk, when we sold the vegetable slicer, we used plenty of humor and lots of funny comparisons. It helps you stay in focus and stay excited. If you are just droning along with the same old pitch, you lose interest in it, and then it gets harder to get somebody else interested.

PSP: *Could you give us an example of how you used humor in your famous Morris Metric Slicer presentations?*

McMahon: Well, for instance, we'd slice a tomato with a knife and say, "Did you ever see a lady slice a tomato? She takes a poor, defenseless tomato and stabs at it with a butcher knife. And the poor little tomato dies of a hemorrhage before it ever reaches the table." Then we'd use the Morris Metric Slicer: "Now watch as I show you how this wonderful little invention handles your tomato problems. Look at those slices. Each one is so thin, it's no wonder stingy people adore this little machine. I sold one of these to a lady in Bayonne, New Jersey, and it made one tomato last her all summer long."

PSP: *I can see you selling hundreds of those machines.*

McMahon: I did.

PSP: *So you are saying that humor helps you stay in focus. Do you feel that there is a relationship between staying in focus and having confidence?*

McMahon: Yes. Focus makes you better at what you are doing. The minute you start getting better, your confidence grows. Once you know that, it's easier the next time.

PSP: *Is it true that Charles Bronson and Jack Klugman learned from your presentations in Atlantic City?*

McMahon: Yes. They worked for my father in what was essentially a bingo game, but it was called SKILLO, because there were some skills involved. They were trying to become mike men. My father would send them down to watch me and listen to my pitch. They had been studying like I did and made money using their voices on a microphone to get where they wanted to go. Atlantic City was a great experience for me because it not only gave me a chance to be selling, but to be very funny in front of a crowd. I had people so excited, they were throwing money at me shouting, "Don't forget me! Don't forget me!"

PSP: *In your autobiography you wrote that W. C. Fields was your idol. What did you learn from him?*

McMahon: He was a master of comic timing—verbal and nonverbal. I have a room in my home which I call the W. C. Fields room, it's the W.C., the water closet. Inside are all kinds of paraphernalia of him, a wood carving on one wall, little statuettes. . . . When you turn on the light, you hear an old Lucky Strike show. I keep changing it, but the one that is running right now can give you an example of how funny he was. He was using words that no other comedian ever used. In the show he's talking backstage and the announcer says, "Mr. Fields, everybody can hear what you're saying. Don't talk until you're introduced." Now his response was [*McMahon tilts his mouth and imitates W. C. Fields' voice*], "The man asked me a civil question. I have to give him a civil answer. My grandfather was a Civil War veteran. I've got a brother who is a civil engineer. It's in the family to be civil." [*Big belly laugh.*] He was one of the greatest jugglers in the world. He did tricks that no one has ever duplicated.

PSP: *You are selling many different products on TV. How many commercials do you do a year?*

McMahon: Between 600 and 800.

PSP: *That's two or three a day.*

McMahon: We do more than that. When we shoot commercials, I come to the studio at 8:00 in the morning and usually I do eight different commercials on eight different sets and I leave at noon.

PSP: *What was your favorite commercial?*

McMahon: A Budweiser commercial with Frank Sinatra that was shot in Florida. We were doing six commercials that day and I was told that "You have Mr. Sinatra for only one hour." We had to be very efficient and I rehearsed the previous day with a stand-in who looked exactly like Sinatra. When Sinatra arrived the next day, everything went like clockwork. He's very efficient and he really knew his lines. In less than one hour we had done five commercials. On the last one, we were cavalry officers, tied to the wheels of an Army wagon, and I was supposed to say, "What do you think got those Indians so upset?" and his copy was, "You, by telling them that the gold they had was unredeemable quartz." But Frank couldn't say "unredeemable." He blew it about six times in a row. He was getting angrier by the minute and everybody was petrified. Before the seventh take, I looked at him with a stern face and said, "Look, Frank, I don't have all day!" and there was this long pause. Then, he exploded with laughter. He was laughing so hard, he had to leave, and was hitting his hands on the side of the studio. I nailed him in front of his cronies. The upshot was that he did it the next time.

PSP: *He redeemed himself.*

McMahon: That's right.

PSP: *You seem to be very cool under pressure. As a Marine fighter pilot, you once landed a plane that had a defective wing.*

McMahon: Yes, I flew a Corsair that had been rebuilt after it had lost a wing. It needed to be tested and the moment I got off the ground I knew there was trouble. I couldn't get the plane into a level position, it remained at about a 45 degree left bank. I didn't want to jump and tried to save the plane. After 11 approaches, I said, "I'm coming in at this pass—regardless." They had everything prepared, the firetrucks . . . the meatwagons. My hands were tired and I mentally shut my eyes and did it.

PSP: *How do you tune out reality consciously?*

McMahon: Good question. I see through the rainbow. I see myself doing it. I focus on that and I get there.

PSP: *You are talking about visualization techniques.*

McMahon: Yes. For example, when I wanted to work in Las Vegas, I saw myself on a Las Vegas stage and went ahead and did it. Of course, it took a while to get there. I developed an act, I honed it and fine-tuned it, and I went all around the country breaking it in. When I walked out on the stage in Vegas, I was successful. They hired me on the spot for another two weeks, and later hired me for the season.

PSP: *Did you use visualization techniques in selling too?*

McMahon: Sure. You need to see the finished situation. When we used to sell the slicer, there was a certain point where you entice them by saying, "All right, who is going to be number one?" Then you see someone responding and you say, "Yes, hold your hand up high, you're number one!" Once you are at that point, you see people with their dollars way up high in the air. "All right, who will be the second person?" You see that happening and all you have to do is to take the dollar and hand them the merchandise as fast as you can.

PSP: *You anticipate the positive event.*

McMahon: Yes, it's the same with the warm-up at "The Tonight Show." After I get a few laughs from the audience, the next thing I want to get is my big laugh. That first, real, big laugh that they did not want to give me. I know it's coming. I'm waiting for it. I know where it's going to be and I go for it. You have to see the finished product of your efforts.

PSP: *Do you feel you had a tough time as a kid?*

McMahon: I had a very lonely childhood because we were moving around so much. I never knew anybody. I never had any friends. That bothered me a lot. Now that I know how gregarious I am and how much friends mean to me, I realize how terrible a void that was.

PSP: *A void that became the cradle of ambition.*

McMahon: Very good point.

PSP: *Do you feel you were not accepted when you changed schools and neighborhoods so quickly?*

McMahon: Yes. I remember when I went to a high school in Philadelphia, there were 5,000 students and I didn't know a soul. I got on a trolley every morning and went to school across town and no one said hello to me until May. That's a long time. I was into myself all that time. That's when I was practicing being a radio announcer using a flashlight as a mike in my grandmother's dining room.

PSP: *But you turned your dreams into reality.*

McMahon: Yes. When I began to blossom, I really blossomed. I went after it all.

PSP: *What's your definition of success?*

McMahon: To set some wish on fire.

PSP: *How?*

McMahon: Take something you want and get it so heated and boiling, that it will get you going until you get it.

Ed McMahon's
Timeless Sales Magic

by Dr. Donald J. Moine

Ed McMahon is a sales superstar. I know. I've had the opportunity to spend time with and work with some of the best—people making $500,000, $1 million, or more per year, take home. If he wasn't in the entertainment business, Ed could make that in sales.

His autobiography, *Here's Ed,* contains a fascinating account of Ed's awesome sales powers in action. The scene is the Atlantic City boardwalk. The time is just after World War II.

The range and sequencing of sales strategies Ed used were phenomenal. No one could resist his charm, his wit, his surprises, his honesty. The setting seems somewhat unique, but it could have been *anywhere.* People are people. These persuasion principles have universal application.

On the left are Ed's exact words. On the right, we present an X-ray look at what makes them so powerful. This is the art of sales magic as performed by one of its greatest practitioners:

"The Tonight Show" in 2014

Ed's Pitch	Analysis
"I'm about to sell ten of these empty boxes."	*Creates surprise and the need to understand.*
". . . just exactly ten . . . the specially selected ten I have piled up right here on the counter. . . ."	*Ed triggers scarcity thinking: there are only ten!*
"I'm about to sell these ten boxes only to ten lucky buyers for only one dollar each."	*Hypnotically repeats his earlier surprising statement!*
"Now, I hear you saying, 'Who's going to pay a buck for an empty box?' "	*Ed reads their minds.*
"That's a good question."	*Flattery power.*
"Not your staid, conservative, solid unimaginative man with no romance in his soul."	*Uses the power of the mild insult.*
"But those of you who know that there's often more to a thing than meets the eye . . . those of you who can become fascinated, intrigued by an idea . . . those of you who wonder why a man would stand up here before you and offer an empty box for a dollar. . . ."	*Seduction power: flattery and romancing the prospect.*
"You will say to yourself. 'There must be more here than meets the eye.' "	*Ed reads the people's minds.*
"But there is a limit to the number of these empty boxes that I can sell at the price of just one dollar."	*Curiosity power causes the listeners to wonder "why, why, why?" They have to stay to learn!*

Ed's Pitch	Analysis
"Here they are. I will count them for you . . . one, two, three, four, five, six, seven, eight, nine, and ten! That's the limit."	*Presents an undeniably truthful statement, plus visual involvement as he points, plus scarcity thinking!*

[In his book, Ed then comments, "At this point, I would pick up one of the boxes, look knowingly inside it, and smile provocatively at the crowd as if I wished they could see what I saw." This, Ed correctly points out, was acting.]

Ed's Pitch	Analysis
"Now, ladies and gentlemen, I say . . . I say . . . these boxes are empty. That's what I say."	*Uses hypnotic repetition: "Say, say, say."*
"But I wonder if there are ten ladies and gentlemen among you out there who believe that I would actually presume to sell you an empty box."	*Triggers the powerful motivator of human curiosity.*
"So this is what I'm going to do."	*Ed predicts his own behavior.*
"As each of you steps forward to buy one of these little jewelry boxes . . ."	*Assumptive close: Ed assumes they will buy.*
". . . I'm going to put one— the one you buy—on top of your dollar. When I have ten dollars covered by ten boxes, I'm going to ask each of you to step up here, open the box you bought, and find out if I told you the truth when I said the box was empty."	*Ed predicts his own behavior, which fosters suspense-building power.*

Ed's Pitch	Analysis
"Remember, I *say* these boxes are empty. Do you or don't you believe me?"	*Uses hypnotic repetition plus the power of the challenge.*

[Ed would, in almost no time at all, have ten boxes on top of ten one-dollar bills!]

Ed's Pitch	Analysis
"Now then, folks, I want each of you to step up here, open your box, and show everyone here exactly what you bought."	*Does what he predicted he would do: the "yes" set.*
"You bought an empty box, exactly as I told you you would. Very well, ladies and gentlemen, what does that prove? It proves that I am an absolutely honest man."	*Leads the people to believe he is an honest man. He could have just said it, but it is much more powerful to prove it!*
"So you must believe me when I tell you that the very greatest item I have ever been authorized to offer here on the boardwalk of Atlantic City is this handy Morris Metric Slicer which . . ."	*Leads the audience to their next belief, that this is the greatest product!*
". . . I have here in my hand."	*Uses visual involvement.*
"Forget the $2 these great little gadgets were made to sell for."	*Uses curiosity power to make people ask, "Why forget?"*
"I'm cutting the price in half. Just look at the way it slices these cucumbers, ladies and gentlemen."	*Uses the power of the bargain plus visual involvement.*
"Is that great or is that sensational?"	*Forced-choice close: Either way, Ed wins!*

Ed's Pitch	Analysis
"With a machine like this, you can slice anything, so thin, you could get a job with a tobacco company slicing calling cards into cigarette papers."	*Sells with word pictures.*
"And I'm about to give this little machine more use and abuse in the next two minutes than you would give it in an entire lifetime."	*Uses the power of the challenge, plus the power of curiosity: "What will he do with it?" They must stay!*
"It's guaranteed not to rip, rust, bust, split in the back, or smell bad in warm weather."	*Uses the power of the guarantee, plus humor power.*
"Just a minute, what was that I heard? Did someone say cabbage? Thank you. Perfect stranger. Get a load of how this remarkable little machine handles your cabbage problems."	*Uses the power of the (self-imposed) challenge and need-building power: describes cabbage as a "problem."*
"For coleslaw, hot slaw, sauerkraut, or anything that may constitute your cabbage pleasure. Could I hear it for this coleslaw, ladies and gentlemen?"	*Uses the power of word pictures and the power of humor in selling: Cabbage "problem" has been changed to "pleasure."*
"But wait a minute, that's not all!"	*Suspense-building statement.*
"Did you ever see a lady slice a tomato? She takes a poor defenseless tomato and plunges at it with a butcher knife. And the poor little to-*	*Uses the power of word pictures plus the power of sales humor.*

Ed's Pitch	Analysis
mato dies of a hemorrhage before it ever reaches the table."	
"Now watch as I show you how this wonderful little invention handles your tomato problem."	*Ed predicts his own behavior and hypnotically repeats vegetable "problem" theme, thus uniting the sales presentation.*
"Look at those slices, ladies and gentlemen. Each one is so thin, it's no wonder stingy people adore this little machine.	*Visually focusses audience's attention to keep them from straying. Plus, acts as a humorous appeal to their desire to save money ("stingy").*
"Why I sold one of these to a lady in Bayonne, New Jersey, and it made one tomato last her all summer long."	*Uses repetitious sales humor. People are laughing so much now they can't help but like Ed (and his product).*
"Look at those slices!"	*Visually focusses audience's attention.*
"And . . . wait a minute, ladies and gentlemen, that's not all!"	*Suspense-building statement.*
"Today and for today only I'm including with each and every sale of this remarkable slicing machine a rotisserie cutter invented by the famous dean of the Parisian School of Potato Surgery. It was he himself who taught me how to use it."	*Triggers scarcity thinking: "Today and for today only." Also uses more powerful sales humor!*
"Any child can learn."	*Psychological reassurance statement.*

Ed's Pitch	**Analysis**
"Look at this!"	*Attention-focussing statement.*

[At this point, Ed would spin a potato on it and produce a springlike spiral of potato that he'd pull out and let snap back.]

Ed's Pitch	**Analysis**
"When company comes to dinner, spread it out. When they go home, let it snap back together again. One potato could last you a lifetime."	*Uses intoxicating sales humor. At this point, the audience is laughing so much and feeling so good they'd buy anything from Ed!*
"And in addition to the slicer and the machine for performing miracles with a potato, I'm adding the juice-o-matic . . . here it is folks . . . all for one dollar."	*Appeals to bargain-hunting mentality, plus provides sales humor.*
"Plunge this handy little juice-o-matic into an orange, a grapefruit, or a watermelon like this."	*Uses visual involvement and attention-focussing.*
"Take it with you on your way to work and drink the juice right out of the fruit on your way downtown."	*Uses the selling power of word pictures.*
"We don't supply the vodka."	*Still more sales humor!*
"Stick this into a lemon and you have juice for a salad, a little lemon for your Tom Collins, and some for Mary and Jane Collins, too. There's enough for the whole damn Collins family."	*More sales humor! Ed has us laughing so much, we have forgotten all of our worldly problems.*

Ed's Pitch	Analysis
"And wait till you try it on a grapefruit. Take this number two grapefruit. With this juice-o-matic you get enough juice to float the USS North Dakota."	*More sales humor. At this point, I like Ed so much, I want him to be my son-in-law!*
"Who'll be the first to raise her hand and say, "I'll be the first to give you a dollar for these three marvelous kitchen innovations?"	*Ed uses the power of hypnotic suggestion and tells them what to say!*
"Lady over there? Thank you very much, my dear. And there's a man who wants two. He's obviously leading a double life, the sly old fox. Good luck to you, sir. And thank you all for your enthusiasm. You have made this sale a success for all of us. And to those of you who didn't buy, I hope you won't regret the mistake too much in the future when you might want to become a little cut-up."	*Uses a play on words: "cut-up" (what his product does).*

As the crowd wandered away, Ed would start his pitch again, always beginning with the empty boxes to show how truthful he was. No one ever complained about the boxes because no sucker wants to be caught in the act of sounding like one. Ed made 400 percent profit on everything he sold, plus the dollar on the empty box was free and clear. Nobody ever took the box he or she bought! It was a wonderful summer job and Ed earned enough money to register at Catholic University in

Washington, D.C., to study drama. Sales made it all possible. And, this same sales presentation would undoubtedly be just as effective if performed today. Try it yourself!

McMahon's sales pitch was excerpted from his autobiography *Here's Ed*, copyright © 1976 by Ed McMahon. Reprinted by permission of G.P. Putnam's Sons, New York, N.Y.

3

Sunny-Weather Sales
Ron Rice

"I was driven to the point where I had to work physically and mentally all day long. I had to load the trucks myself, write the invoices, do everything before I could feel comfortable about going home at night."

Driving fast cars, sponsoring giant sporting events, organizing bathing beauty contests—it all looks like so much hype that one can almost imagine Ron Rice as a sort of Tropical Svengali of suntan. But this image belies the serious, purposeful, hard-working bachelor behind the lotions that make beaches and ski slopes from Hawaii to Malibu, from Daytona Beach to St. Tropez, radiate with tans. If disappointment is the stuff from which future business success springs, then Rice's entrepreneurial figure was outlined in early childhood.

When we drove to Daytona Beach, where Hawaiian Tropic's corporate headquarters is located, we expected a certain degree of casual corporate style. But we weren't fully prepared for the Kon Tiki version of managerial mastery that greeted us. The entrance to the low buildings that make up Hawaiian Tropic's corporate headquarters is flanked by 10-foot-high hand-carved island totems. On arriving Friday afternoon, we were immediately impressed by the two black Porsches parked outside the main entrance with license plates that read Tropic 1 and Tropic 2.

Upon entering the building, our eyes were met by a floor-to-ceiling display of photos showing company president and founder Rice with countless celebrities from all the more glamorous walks of life. The only sight that had more impact, especially on male visitors, was the receptionist, dressed in short shorts, stiletto heels, and a tee shirt (braless), with a glass of white wine in her hand. To her left, a garbage can mounted on a platform stood as silent testimony to the very first batch of Hawaiian Tropic Ron Rice had mixed and bottled by hand in his garage.

We were told that Friday is a half-day for most of the company's employees, the oldest of whom at that time was 24. In characteristic Rice style, the company is run on the theory that happy employees produce better work—that employees who are responsible to and for themselves will be more attentive to their tasks, and will therefore make fewer mistakes and fewer bad decisions. (One of the hardest things for Rice to do, he confided to us, was to give up the reins for even a moment and let someone else make the mistakes that eventually lead to success.)

Rice's private office was unlike any other we have ever seen. The conference chairs could have been created for a Viking feast. Carved out of tree trunks, with the largest limb protruding as a desktop surface for writing or resting one's arm, they were covered with plush lamb skins. A large painting of the president's Lamborghini Countach graced one wall and a giant chess set carved from stone was set on a table cum checkerboard that served as the conference table. Rice's own desk, of inch-thick glass and covered with mementos, was surprisingly free from paperwork clutter. The telephone was nearby, and rang continually.

For all the carefree atmosphere and freewheeling open communication between executive, clerical, and production personnel, this is a business run with efficiency and order. Rice knows exactly where he stands at all times. And he knows where everyone else stands as well. We were given a tour of the company game room. "We like to play sometimes— competition is healthy," explained Rice, a former high school coach and chemistry teacher. Then Rice treated us to a ride in his Porsche, taking time to stop off at his home on the Atlantic, where he houses his famous $250,000 Lamborghini Countach (which appeared in such films as "Cannonball Run").

Ron still works long days, but only because that's what he enjoys. He is long past the time when the competition is trying to squeeze him out of the market, the time when selling suntan lotion was a pool-deck-by-pool-deck affair. Now his products appear in department stores, drug stores, chains of motel gift shops, and every surf shop in the nation.

Ron Rice mixed his first batch of Hawaiian Tropic suntan lotion by hand in a galvanized trash can in his garage in 1967. In 1984 his company, with $70 million in sales, was number two in the world. In this exclusive interview with Personal Selling Power, *Ron speaks with candor, humor,*

and pride about his company, his humble beginnings, work, persever-
ance, selling, and success.

Hawaiian Tropic's mix of business and pleasure creates an enviable
working climate where the laid-back atmosphere belies the talent and
determination behind his incredible success story. Descriptions of the
sporting events and beauty pageants sponsored by this Daytona-based
empire read like a celebrity Who's Who, including such names as Burt
Reynolds, Cheryl Tiegs, John Denver, Paul Newman, and many others.

Despite this dizzying array of stars, Ron Rice is still tied to the basic
American values he learned as a youngster: honesty, fair play, tough
competition, and lots of hard work. They have led to unprecedented
success for this lifeguard-turned-suntan-lotion tycoon.

PSP: *What was your original idea behind Hawaiian Tropic?*
Rice: I had gone to Hawaii, and I saw that the women on the
beach were using homemade suntanning formulas with coconut and avocado oils. So when I came home, I started mixing
the first products by trial and error in a trash can in my garage.
I hired some teenagers to bottle the lotion by hand and took it
to the lifeguards at the beach to try it out.

PSP: *What was your original investment?*
Rice: I borrowed $500 from my father. At that time I was a
teacher making $4,000 a year, and another $300 coaching
football. I also worked as a lifeguard in the summertime. I was
always looking for something extra.

PSP: *So your only risk was $500?*
Rice: Yes, it was just a matter of being able to sell $500 worth
of products, which I knew I could do.

PSP: *Were you oriented toward business as a youngster?*
Rice: I grew up on top of a mountain in North Carolina. My
older brother is a forest ranger now. I had a lot of business
ventures as a kid. I bred and sold dogs, ran roadside stands;
my father would drop me off in the morning down at the
bottom of the mountain, and I'd sell all day long, and at
nightfall he'd pick me up again and take me home back up the
mountain. I also planted a grape vineyard and sold the grapes,

had beehives and sold the honey, and even made Christmas wreaths. My sister and big brother worked for me. I'd sell, and my brother would carry the product.

PSP: *When did you sell your first bottle of Hawaiian Tropic suntan lotion?*

Rice: In 1966.

PSP: *What was your sales volume in 1983?*

Rice: About $70 million.

PSP: *How do you explain the reasons behind your company's incredible growth?*

Rice: Hard work, luck, and just a lot of good timing. We hit the market at the right time. And we had enough energy to do the job.

PSP: *When you say timing, what do you mean?*

Rice: It was a new, quality item, and it hit the market before the natural products craze. The craze hit hard around the late 1960s. We had the only natural suntan lotion out there at the time. We had a good organization, people liked the image of Hawaii, and they liked the fragrance. The only weak link in the entire organization was that we didn't have much money. But—had I had a lot of money to launch this product, and not started at zero—the product probably wouldn't be where it is right now.

PSP: *What were you like in the beginning?*

Rice: I was driven to the point where I had to work physically and mentally all day long. I had to load the trucks myself, write the invoices, do everything before I could feel comfortable about going home at night. This was back when we had one little building. As a matter of fact [points out the window], it was that little building right there, and that was our thirteenth location around Daytona.

PSP: *When did you know that you really had something?*

Rice: Immediately . . . but not until around three years later did I realize it was going to really grow. Then, about 1973, I knew it was going to be really big. That's when we turned the corner in the market.

PSP: *What was your sales volume in 1973?*

Rice: $4 million. Then it went to $15 million right away. We never could keep up with sales.

PSP: *What selling methods did you use at the start?*

Rice: At that time I had an old Ford Mustang convertible, and the ocean had just about eaten it apart. I just drove around to pool decks and lifeguards and little beach-front mom-and-pop stores, and sold it to them. Even though it wasn't really planned ahead of time it was a smart move to create the demand out at the beach first. After that it went into the high-fashion stores in New York and then into the chain department stores across the country.

PSP: *Did you call on those stores?*

Rice: I did some, and I hired other people by that time who specialized in that.

PSP: *Where did your sales force come from?*

Rice: When I quit teaching and coaching, I brought a lot of teachers and coaches and ex-football players with me. When they saw the business growing, they started dropping off one by one and coming with me. A lot of lifeguards came over, too.

PSP: *How did you get the lifeguards to leave the beach?*

Rice: They saw the potential in it and wanted to move onto something different. Many of them laughed at me then, and some of those are still working at the beach.

PSP: *Are any of your original salespeople still with you?*

Rice: I have one guy who controls the whole western United States. He makes $2 million a year now. He started back here at the beginning. Another one controls the Northeast, and he used to run a little scooter stand here on Daytona Beach.

PSP: *Were your competitors surprised by your success?*

Rice: I remember when there was a turning point in 1973. My competitors finally woke up and realized that we were really going to grow beyond their expectations. And it scared them to death. So they did everything they could to hurt me.

PSP: *What did they do?*

Rice: They sent the government down here to try and stop me. That was a very amusing situation. It was right before the oil prices skyrocketed, and one of the biggest companies in this business hired a team of doctors to write a report—a huge thick thing—and they submitted it to every government agency in Washington, D.C. They listed every possible thing that we could be doing wrong and then they made it sound like we were doing it.

PSP: *What happened next?*

Rice: I got a call on a Wednesday from the FTC in Atlanta. The official said he would come down here on Monday to meet with me and talk about these business problems. I just about panicked. I didn't know what to do. So, I said, "Well, exactly what do you want to talk about?" And he would not tell me. He just said, "You have problems with your business." I didn't have an attorney at the time so I went and talked to a friend. He said, "Yeah, that's serious. These guys can put you out of business." So I contacted my salesman in the Northeast and told him, "We are going up there to some of these government offices and see if we can find out what's going on. We're going to get the jump on 'em."

PSP: *Did you think of getting in touch with your congressman?*

Rice: At that time I didn't even know what a congressman did.

PSP: *So you went to Washington.*

Rice: Yes, the next day we walked from office to office at HEW in Washington. Finally we met a guy who started laughing when we said that we were with Hawaiian Tropic. He said: "It's funny you're here. Look at this book. Somebody gave it to me at a party last night." Then he said, "I can't let you read this book, but I have to go down the hall and talk to somebody. I'll be back in a few minutes."

PSP: *Did you look at it?*

Rice: Yes, I did. I saw the doctors' names and realized what was going on. Surprisingly, the major point they were making was that we didn't use any sunscreens.

PSP: *How did you handle the official from the FTC?*

Rice: When he walked in on Monday morning, I asked him right away, "Are you here because of that report everyone's got a copy of down there in Washington?" And his eyes got real big. I realized that I had just blown his ace in the hole. From that point on he was on the defensive. He had brought his wife and three teenage daughters down with him, and while we were talking they were all by the pool at a big motel over at the beach. He stayed for three days, but what really burned him was that while we were having meetings, one of the lifeguards was selling his wife and daughters $47 worth of our products. He came back the second day just steaming because his wife had spent so much of his money on our product. He recommended that the agency come after us with everything they had, but they turned him down and dropped the whole thing.

PSP: *You were a chemistry teacher before you started. What made you decide to quit teaching?*

Rice: I didn't get along with the administration. I had my own ideas about teaching and motivation, and they didn't like them. I worked in six schools in eight years and got fired five times. I can't work for anyone else. There was just too much busy work. I could do in one hour what it took other people eight hours to do. But if I didn't sit there and look busy—then they didn't think I was working.

PSP: *What ingredient for success did you bring to your new business?*

Rice: Willingness to work. A driven motivation. I was possessed. Sometimes I'd go a whole day without eating and not realize it till the next day.

PSP: *What would you consider your strongest management talent?*

Rice: More than anything else—anticipation. I haven't had the first marketing course or even one business course. I just went strictly by gut reactions. To know ahead of time what you're going to do, you really have to have a keen sense of anticipation. I made a few mistakes as I came along, but I was careful and didn't make a lot of mistakes, and things went well.

PSP: *When you talk about anticipation, did you learn that from your experience with coaching?*

Rice: Yes, I never had a losing team. I would hand each player reports on the player who was going to be opposite him on the line before a game. We had games a week apart. I worked non-stop on planning for a game. I'd go out and scout the other team's players, film them, then watch the film and analyze each player in every situation. Then I'd let my players know what to expect from the other side. That's what it takes to be a successful coach.

PSP: *You mentioned earlier that you made a few mistakes. What mistakes did you make?*

Rice: People were always coming to me and wanting me to invest in new things. Once I went into 13 different businesses. I realized quickly that none of them were any good and I got out real quick.

PSP: *What lessons did you learn from your mistakes?*

Rice: One important thing that I learned is that not everybody is good at everything. For example, take a person who is good at sales, but is not a good money manager. Even if he can do a fantastic job in selling but doesn't manage his money well, then we'll both lose. Another thing I learned was to stick to what I know and what I do best. Persistence is very important for an entrepreneur.

PSP: *What was the toughest thing for you to learn?*

Rice: The hardest thing to learn was delegating authority. I wanted to do everything myself. When I hired employees and started delegating authority, I would see other people making mistakes—and not seeing things that I could see. At first it bugged me. I couldn't understand why they couldn't see it.

PSP: *How did you grow beyond that?*

Rice: I started training people by letting them make their own mistakes and then they learned from them. It was just like helping the moth out of a cocoon. If you help him out, then he doesn't have the strength to fly.

PSP: *How did you become a sponsor of sporting events and beauty contests?*

Rice: We decided to sponsor football teams, basketball teams, ski races—really any kind of sporting event—because they are watched by people who get out in the sun. It has paid off very well. We've had three and sometimes four cars in Le Mans for the past eight years. We've had Paul Newman drive for us. He won the Le Mans in our car in 1978. We've done big promotions with Burt Reynolds. We sponsored the cars in the movie "Cannonball Run." We also sponsor charity tournaments and Olympic training.

PSP: *What's the strategy behind that?*

Rice: It's a real smart media buy. We get a lot of subliminal coverage from all our logos and banners.

PSP: *How do you measure the effects of that?*

Rice: It's hard to measure. It goes back to gut reaction. You know that it's doing some good so you have to put a value on it. You know how much to spend and how much not to spend. You spend as little as possible to get as much coverage as possible.

PSP: *What was your most successful promotion ever?*

Rice: Le Mans has been very successful, but I think the best was the beauty contest we did in 1983. It lasted a week. We had 104 girls from all over the United States. We got fantastic coverage from it.

PSP: *What is the most important quality for a top salesperson in your industry?*

Rice: A good personality and a good sense of humor.

PSP: *Have you ever had an offer to buy you out?*

Rice: I've had 30 or more offers like that over the last three or four years. Revlon tried to buy us out the week before Charles Revson died. That was interesting. We met with them in New York. They are on the 50th floor. When you get off the elevator, there is a long hallway with plush red carpet and beautiful paintings lining the walls. It looks like you're walking through the Louvre. I took six of my key people with me, all young guys, and we were carrying our suitcases with us in order to make a plane connection. When we got off the elevator, the receptionist could see us coming down this long hallway— seven big guys with suitcases. She was about to have a fit. She waved at us, saying, "Get back on the elevator." So we dropped our bags down beside her desk and said, "Isn't this the Revlon hotel?" It was hilarious.

PSP: *Do you feel that you've exceeded your original dreams?*
Rice: As I look back on it now I still cling to the feeling that I didn't really think it was going to develop into this.
PSP: *Did you have doubts?*
Rice: No . . . I didn't even consider it. As it went along and I saw what was developing, then I built the dream. I guess that as a youngster I already had big dreams. I went back to a high school reunion and one of my buddies from school showed me that I had written in his high school annual, "One of these days I'm going to be a millionaire and I'm going to buy you a Corvette." I didn't remember writing that—but I went out and bought a plastic Corvette, about two feet long, and put it in a box and gave it to him.
PSP: *Do you think it's easier to make it in business today?*
Rice: Yes, I do. I see opportunities today that I wouldn't have seen before, but I also understand them now.
PSP: *How many people do you think were trying to start a similar business like yours back in the late 1960s?*
Rice: There were certainly people who started at the same time but they did not make it because they weren't willing to put the hard work into it. And they got diverted off into other things.
PSP: *Isn't the lack of capital the prime reason that causes them to fail?*
Rice: No, it's not the money. It's the hard work. That's what it boils down to.
PSP: *Other than hard work, to what do you attribute your success?*
Rice: Reading people—and understanding human nature.
PSP: *To what degree do you feel that luck was a contributing factor?*
Rice: My luck was in timing and hitting the market at the right time. Just about the time that my product was coming onto the market, another company was advertising a product called Tanya. Their product was only on the shelves in Hawaii and there were three things they advertised all over the United States: Hawaii, coconut oil, and Tanya. Well, we were already

in the market, and we had Hawaii and coconut oil, so people bought our product. It was selling so fast I couldn't keep it on the shelves. We also had great packaging. Nobody spends the money on packaging that we do.

PSP: *What's your measure of success?*

Rice: Being happy. Some people measure it in money. I'm happy that I've been able to help a lot of other people.

PSP: *What do you feel is the price of success?*

Rice: Having a lot on your mind. But I always want to have a challenge. A lot of people spend all their time worrying over money and then all their time is used up. All you've got is time. That's all there is.

PSP: *You have been labeled the Hugh Hefner of Daytona Beach.*

Rice: I do like to enjoy myself. Back in the beginning all the guys at the beach tried to get me to go out and drink with them while I was trying to build a business. Now they're working and I'm playing.

PSP: *You were playing ping-pong in the company game room when we first arrived. Who is the best ping-pong player in the company?*

Rice: Well, there was one guy who could beat me, but I fired him [he chuckles]. No, I encouraged him to go out on his own, and he's done very well for himself. You've got to listen to your own instincts and take advantage when an opportunity comes along. That's what it's all about.

Ron Rice and the Oil Salesman

"We use a lot of oil to make our products. One day a sales executive for one of the largest oil companies in the world called on me. Since I had been a coach, and his son had gone to play at Georgia Tech, he figured that he was going to sell his oil to me.

"But his price was higher than anyone else's and he couldn't understand why I wouldn't buy from him. It got to be an obsession with him.

"One day he got angry and warned me, 'If you don't buy from me now, when the bad times come and the sources dry up, I'll make sure that you don't get any oil.'

"Then the oil crisis hit. I quickly took the initiative and I told my distributors to go out and buy oil anywhere they could.

"One of my guys in the Northeast lucked into a situation where there was a whole railyard of oil that had been sitting for awhile. He opened an account and bought one trailer load one day and another one the next. During a few weeks, he bought over 30 trailer loads. We received a continuous load of oil down here.

"Finally, we must have had 1,000 drums in our inventory. When we saw we had enough, we sat back.

"Now a few days later, in walks the oil salesman, who by now had gotten downright vindictive. He came in with a big grin on his face and he said, 'I suppose you want some oil, don't you?' I said, 'No, I don't need any oil. In fact, I'll sell you some. How much do you need?' Then I made up a story about how I'd really had a stroke of luck while I was vacationing in the Middle East. I said that I had met an oil sheik in a bar and really hit if off with his son. He just sent me a whole boat load of oil. I made the story good and believable, and he just stormed out.

"I remember, I was wearing a bright red shirt that day. I went out to the stockyard and saw him by the fence copying down numbers off the drums. When he saw my red shirt, he took off and I haven't seen him since."

You Are What You Drive

Forty-two-year old Ron Rice's personal net worth of about $15 million allows this former lifeguard to make whatever statement he wants, car-wise. Along with driving his $40,000 Porsche Turbo and 1978 Silver Anniversary Issue Corvette, Rice also enjoys cruising the tropical avenues of Daytona Beach in his Lamborghini Countach S, a forty-one-inch high

bolt of black lightning with a price tag of $250,000. The Countach (pronounced coon-tash) usually costs somewhere around $120,000, give or take $10,000. But for Ron Rice, this car is extra special.

Clocked by Las Vegas police during the filming of the Burt Reynolds movie "Cannonball Run" at 227 m.p.h., Rice's Countach (which in Italian slang means "Oh my God") has special modifications for high *high* performance. Extras include two telephones, two radar detectors, a powerful CB radio, special switches for extra lighting, and a switch to douse all rear lights to deter nocturnal police tracking.

The symbol Italian designer Signor Ferricuio picked for his Lamborghini is the bull: powerful, hard driving, and macho; it is an apt choice. With few Countach owners in this country, those who drive them comprise a rare breed like Rice and publishing tycoon Malcolm Forbes.

The low aggressive-looking Countach with its aircraftlike stabilizing wings at front and rear and its V-12 engine, which spins out 600 h.p. at 8,000 r.p.m.'s, is the perfect match for a laid-back fun-in-the-sun beauty pageant backer who speaks with a slow drawl and doesn't quit until he crosses the finish line—first, of course.

4

The Art of Persuasion

Tony Schwartz

"I do best with products where I can let people know about the things they need. I tell them about what products can do and then they make their own decisions."

In the field of persuasion Tony Schwartz occupies a unique position. He can sell soap and political candidates with equal ease, and when asked how he persuades so convincingly, he answers with a smile, "I don't use manipulation at all. I think it is better to get people to do things for their own reasons." When we first decided to interview Schwartz, our reasons were simple. He has been responsible for some very revolutionary concepts in the field of persuasion. It is around the foundation that he and Marshall McLuhan created together that our media-oriented society now functions.

Ideas like the global village, communicating through media, and persuading by leaving things out rather than by dense packing of information—suggest only a smattering of the concepts that Tony Schwartz initiated. During the interview he talked about the hard sell, the soft sell, and—his sell—the deep sell. Schwartz uses his knowledge of how our minds function, along with his extraordinary facility with media, to sell deep into the "nonconscious" (Schwartz prefers this to unconscious) mind.

Schwartz is not an easy-going person. One senses his intensity and questioning nature immediately. He has no interest in flattering or cajoling. It seems to make little difference to him whether he's easy or hard to work with. He doesn't measure success by the number of goods sold by any one of his ads. He is interested in people's motives. He looks for what makes them move. He investigates their underlying needs and desires. Then he goes to his laboratory, the sound studio, to develop new ways to reach them.

Schwartz owns two buildings next to each other on New York's West Side and has broken through their shared wall for easy access. We arrived just as a famous politician was leaving and a well-known radio announcer was arriving. The walls of Schwartz's office are plastered with memorabilia. His office is also his studio, where thousands of commercials a year are taped and edited by this master of the media. (Schwartz, who suffers from agoraphobia, rarely goes out and never travels far beyond a few blocks from his home—anyone who wants to meet with or work with him goes to his home.)

The day of our appointment was particularly hectic because Schwartz had just been interviewed for a national news spot that was to be aired that evening. The newscaster and necessary camera and sound crews, with their equipment, wires, and cables strewn about, created an atmosphere that was hardly conducive to the quiet interview and reflective afternoon we had hoped for. But, like a storm that blows in and then vanishes, the newscast chaos was soon gone and we sat down to talk.

There's a lot to be learned from this man, but he does not offer a facile kind of quick mental fix. He is not interested in motivating us. He has made a significant contribution to contemporary society and can help us know more thoroughly who we are. He is therefore worth our attention.

Tony Schwartz is busy selling—making an impact that is felt all over the country from an unimposing brownstone in a not-too-fashionable section of Manhattan's West Side. He's been doing it for decades. But he rarely leaves his office, which is also his home. Schwartz is a media genius. Though you may not know his face, at some time one of his TV or radio ads has surely precipitated your decision to buy. Tony Schwartz is the man called in to make the media pitch for a range of products, from cold cream to Dream Whip, from Democrat to Republican. In some cases, his political ads have received so much attention that the opposing forces in the campaign had to change strategy in midstream.

As Schwartz stated in an interview with the Washington Post, *"I was the first one to do commercials for the American Cancer Society dealing with emotions rather than medical facts." He was likewise the first to use a real child's voice in a commercial rather than follow tradition and use a woman imitating a child. And he claims the educators are mistaken in fighting television; he believes they should be using it.*

Schwartz has written eloquently about the media, post-literate society, TV, radio, commercials, and a host of other topics in his books, Media, The Second God *(Doubleday Anchor Books: Garden City, N.Y., 1983) and* The Responsive Chord *(Doubleday Anchor Books: Garden City, N.Y., 1974). He has appeared, via satellite, on the "Phil Donahue Show," has been interviewed and quoted widely, and was the subject of an hour-long Bill Moyers' special on PBS.*

Schwartz is a pioneer whom many call a genius. Together with Marshall McLuhan, he developed many of the media techniques we take for granted today, and he continues in his quests for the new truths in media. He is a practical intellectual—a rare spirit who approaches his own sales record in an offhand way.

As Schwartz himself says, "I don't use manipulation. I use partipu-lation. *I let people know about the things they need and they make their own decisions."*

In this exclusive PSP *interview Tony Schwartz, media mastermind, shares his unique approach to selling. "I don't go for the hard sell or the soft sell," he says, "I go for the deep sell."*

PSP: *How many radio and TV commercials have you created?*

Tony Schwartz: I would say over 20,000. I like to say that I've written more best sellers than anyone else in the world.

PSP: *One of the things you're so well known for is your ability to surface feelings, conflicts, and emotions through your radio commercials. How do you do that?*

Schwartz: I have found that anything you can do with pictures you can also do with sound. Let's take a normal Dream Whip commercial. The script reads, "Dream Whip—only 14 calories per tablespoon." Usually this line will be given a literal reading. But I ask, "What is the announcer really saying? He's really saying. "You don't have to worry if you eat Dream Whip. You won't get fat." So, you want to use what I call an environmental reading—a reading that relates to the real world, the world we live in. You want to read it like a woman who's on a diet sharing the news with a fat friend. "Dream Whip has only 14 calories per tablespoon!" Or take Bufferin for another example. "Got a headache? Come to Bufferin." You need to read it like "Got a headache? Come to Mama." That's one level.

PSP: *Is that an unconscious level?*

Schwartz: I don't like the word unconscious. I prefer the word nonconscious. For instance, if you asked me to name all the tapes in my office, I could tell you maybe 500 or 1,000. Then suppose you said, "But what about that one with the man from India? I'd say, "Oh yes. I remember that one." I just wouldn't have been conscious of it.

PSP: *How do you evoke a feeling from the listener?*

Schwartz: It has to do with the difference between learned recall and evoked recall. For example, when my mother went to a store with a shopping list, the storekeeper would take her order, then go back and get the stuff and come out. Radio and TV advertising eliminated the need for the salesclerk and made the stockroom into the store. When you walk through and see the various items, you can say, "Hey, we're out of cereal." Commercials evoke the connection of the product to your life, and once you're in the store, the products evoke both the commercial and your own experience.

PSP: *Can the same techniques you use in commercials be used in person-to-person selling?*

Schwartz: They are all the time. People in all areas of life use them.

PSP: *In your book,* Media, The Second God, *you wrote that you use customers as a work force. What do you mean by that?*

Schwartz: Here's an example. *[Plays a tape of a commercial.]* "You know, there are two men running for Congress in the 6th district. Bob Carr and Charles Chamberlain. Mr. Chamberlain has been in Congress for over 12 years. Let me read you a list of things he's accomplished. *[Dead silence on the tape for a few seconds.]* You see—that's exactly why this message is paid for by a growing number of Republicans and Democrats who want Robert Carr elected to Congress." Presearch* had showed that only one person in a hundred could remember one thing that Chamberlain had done in 12 years in Congress. So I used the audience as a work force. I let them participate in the commercial.

*Editor's note: Presearch, briefly defined, is research conducted before the actual broadcast of a commercial.

PSP: *How would you describe this process?*

Schwartz: I'm allowing people's associations, or lack of associations, to surface. This enables them to use those associations as part of their thinking. Another factor that I find fantastic in communication is shame. It was the most effective means of social control in primitive cultures. I used it in many commercials.

PSP: *Can we hear an example?*

Schwartz: Yes. *[Plays tape.]* Listen to this commercial. "Let me ask you something. Have you ever seen someone allow his dog to go on the sidewalk? Sometimes right in front of a doorway, maybe your doorway? Did it make you angry? Well, don't get angry at the poor soul. Feel sorry for him. He's just a person who's not able to train his dog. He's just not capable of it. In fact, after he's had his dog for a short time, what happens? The dog trains him. So the next time you see a person like that on the street, take a good look at him and while you're looking, feel sorry for him because you know he just can't help himself, even though he might like to. Some people are strong enough and smart enough to train their dogs to take a few steps off the sidewalk. Other people aren't. Makes you wonder, doesn't it, if the master is at the top of the leash or the bottom of the leash." Most people would have said, "You shouldn't let your dog do this." But I said, "You shouldn't should on people." Then I thought, "What could I do to make this person not let his dog do this?" People don't like to be told that they should do something. You're much better off if you can cause them to do it for their own reasons.

PSP: *Isn't that a form of manipulation?*

Schwartz: I don't think the word is accurate. *Partipulation* is the word I'd use to describe the process. A group of people once told me that they don't pay any attention to TV commercials. I asked them what kind of toothpaste they used. They all said Crest. At that time Crest was only being advertised on TV. Partipulating is when the listener becomes an active part of the selling process.

PSP: *You have studied sounds for many years. From the listener's point of view, when does sound become noise?*

Schwartz: Long before the Electronic Age, when someone heard a drunk coming home singing, it used to be sound. When Barbra Streisand singing on the radio became more interesting, then the drunk became noise. Just interchange the word noise for the word sound and you find the real meanings. For instance, the noise of children—the sound of children. People often talk of the clutter factor on radio, but I have no problem with that. If I presearch people's interests, I know what will reach them. If I also do a media profile of the people I presearch, I know what stations they listen to, what magazines they read, and so on. I know what they will mentally tune in to and what they will tune out.

PSP: *Do you think that the media shapes our expectations?*

Schwartz: No. I don't. I think that it fulfills them. When kids watch TV they get a good feeling when they see things they use. "We eat that cereal. Mom drives that car."

PSP: *Who created the "deep sell?"*

Schwartz: I did. I say I'm not interested in hard or soft sell. I'm interested in deep sell. Sometimes deep may come from hard, sometimes from soft. For instance, people don't remember radio as a source of information the way they do newspaper or magazines. They may not consciously listen to radio. They bathe in it—are surrounded by it—in the same way that people at home may have the soap operas on TV while they do their chores. I call this a surround. People hear what relates to their experience and interest, therefore participation is deep into their mind. That's one example of deep sell.

PSP: *In an interview with Bill Moyers you said that no one has experience with answers to problems. They only have experience with the problems. What did you mean by that?*

Schwartz: We talked about creating commercials for politicians. Often people think that the politicians should use commercials to give answers to problems. First, the politicians don't have answers. Second, if they gave the answers, people couldn't identify with the commercials because they don't have experience with the answers—only the problems. So the best commercial is one that makes people feel that the candidate is qualified, and once they feel he or she is capable and qualified, then you want them to feel that the candidate feels the same way they do about the problem.

PSP: *What does that do to the listener?*

Schwartz: When the politician tells how he feels about the problem, the response is, "He feels the same way I do about that—he'll do the right thing."

PSP: *What are your ethical standards in creating a commercial?*

Schwartz: I would never do anything to anyone else that I wouldn't like done to me. I wouldn't do certain ads. I wouldn't do cigarette ads or any ads for a candidate who was opposed to a mutually verifiable nuclear freeze.

PSP: *What's your measure of success?*

Schwartz: Personally, I think being able to earn a living and bring up my family and buy the things that they need. To be a good neighbor and a good person. I do as much free work as I do paid work.

PSP: *What's your professional measure of success?*

Schwartz: I'm very interested in using media for social change. I did a campaign in Massachusetts two years ago to help the state government make up for what Reagan cut out of the budget for aid to education for students. I got $34 million two years ago for student aid for education. Last year I did it again and got $50 million for the same thing. I do work for the hospitals here in New York City, for the fire department and for the police.

PSP: *Do you derive meaning from positive social change?*

Schwartz: Yes. The school across the street was voted out of existence. I thought it was an important school—it was training the police and fire fighters. So I did a campaign and we saved the school.

PSP: *In your book you quoted Daniel Boorstin, "Technology is a way of multiplying the unnecessary." Then you added, "Technology in advertising creates progress by developing the need for the unnecessary." Do you feel you dedicate your life to creating needs for the unnecessary?*

Schwartz: No, I'm not doing that. Maybe some people are

selling products that people don't need. I attach to real things in people. I do best with products where I can let people know about the things they need. I tell them about what products can do and then they make their own decisions.

The "Stanley" Commercial

According to Tony Schwartz, one of the most powerful forms of social control in primitive societies was shame. He believes that shame also works in our new electronic "global village." To illustrate this point for our editors, he played the following tape of one of his well-known commercials (the "Stanley" commercial), read by a sexy-sounding 25-year-old woman.

"You know what Stanley says? He says we can't buy a sofa on Sunday. Stanley says it's alright if we want to buy a sailboat, but a crib and a baby carriage—out. Can't buy 'em. You know what else Stanley says? He says we can buy an antique chair—we need a kitchen chair but Stanley says we can't buy that. You don't know who Stanley is? Stanley Steingut, the New York State Assembly speaker. He's backing a law which will close the department stores and supermarkets on Sunday. Stanley wants the blue laws back again. You want to call Stanley? I'll give you his number. 518/555-3100. I'm glad you're calling. If Stanley knows how you feel about it, maybe he'll change his mind. Paid for by the New York State Retailers Coalition to continue Sunday shopping. Tell Stanley how you feel. 518/555-3100."

[As Schwartz gleefully tells it, "The day after this commercial was aired on the radio, Stanley had to change his office phone number, and his mind!"]

5

Silken Sales
Pak Melwani

"The number one critic of our product is the customer. When a customer says something, we have to jump."

A catalog of silk clothing caught my eye one morning as I was opening the day's mail. It presented lovely silk fashions at the most reasonable prices I had seen and piqued my curiousity about the person behind such an innovative concept. I called the company's headquarters, spoke briefly with the vice-president, and set up an interview with company founder and president Pak Melwani. Royal Silk products—shirts, sweaters, slacks, skirts, and scarves—are now worn regularly by our staff. And the company that energetic entrepreneur Melwani heads is going stronger and moving into new markets even as you read.

Pak is truly an international manager. Today, his operations span the Pacific, from Japan and China for silk and fabric printing, to India for the natural blends we Westerners love to wear, and back to the United States for catalog distribution. If it sounds complicated, it is. To set such an operation in motion takes a very special blend of abilities and disciplines. The language and cross-cultural barriers alone would be enough to stop many. Melwani has added to his particular set of skills the ability to maneuver his corporate ship on foreign waters with an enviable ease.

Sailing was not always so smooth. In the course of Melwani's varied life experience, he has had his share of disappointing experiences and setbacks. It was, indeed, through these that he developed his approach: watching for signs of what the market wants, systematically supplying it, and taking the risks necessary to grow and prosper. Pak is a total professional who suffered the hard knocks of the entrepreneurial risk-taker many times before establishing his present success record. In fact, he had one company that was so undercapitalized it went broke before it got much of a chance to get its feet wet.

No matter. Melwani applied characteristic logic and planning, took a page from his selling lesson book, and looked at what the market might demand in the way of an all-around women's silk shirt. He and a partner (long ago bought out by the farsighted Pak) came up with the safari shirt and advertised it in upscale women's magazines. The skyrocketing success that followed surprised even the young and hopeful Pak, who went on to form his present growing empire.

Pak struck me as a solid, management-oriented executive who would rather take a risk today than rely on successes from yesterday to carry him through. He calculates the odds, and if they are at all favorable he will jump. His selling attitude is one of exceedingly careful respect for the consumers he serves. He stays light on his corporate feet to respond to any changes in market demands. Pak Melwani is a perfect example of the way growth after disappointment can turn a hard lesson from life into a successful achievement.

Pak Melwani was raised in three different countries: India, his native land; Japan, where he spent much of his boyhood and was educated in an international school in Kobe; and the United States, where he was graduated from Columbia University in New York City. He speaks six languages, including English, French, Japanese, and his native Hindi. His smooth-as-silk selling approach currently clothes his company, Royal Silk, in luxurious sales of $22 million a year.

During his school years in Kobe, Pak tutored other students to make ends meet. Later, he financed college studies in New York by working as a waiter and selling magazine subscriptions. Pak reflects on those early days with characteristic optimism: "Being a waiter taught me how to deal with stress, and selling subscriptions helped me to get past all the ego problems most salespeople have. After experiences like that, rejection just doesn't bother me."

Today, Pak Melwani's company, Royal Silk, is an astonishing story of growth. In 1983, its fifth year of business, it was listed number 21 on Inc. Magazine's prestigious 500 Fastest Growing Companies list. According to Melwani, the ability to make it in sales depends on a person's "ability to withstand the numbers." As he puts it, "The numbers are always against you. You just cannot sell on every call you make. What I do is try to be the best I can and learn as much as possible."

In this exclusive interview with PSP, Pak Melwani tells the story of one selling idea and two silk shirts that led him from rags to riches.

PSP: *Is Royal Silk the first business you ever started?*
Melwani: Oh, no. I began with a retail store in New York City that bombed because we were completely undercapitalized. We just couldn't hold out. The concept, the product, and the location were all good, the store had all the right things— except the right amount of money. It was very, very frustrating.
PSP: *How did you start Royal Silk?*
Melwani: I secured a short-term loan of $13,500 and my partner did the same. He then ordered shirts from his father-in-law in India. This was the silk shirt that started the whole ball rolling.

PSP: *When you decide to sell a product, do you see a need and set out to fill it, or do you create the need first?*

Melwani: We do both. In the beginning we accidentally filled an existing need. You have to fulfill some need somewhere. As you get more established, you can then create a need.

PSP: *How did you come to choose silk?*

Melwani: Since silk has always been viewed as a rare and exclusive fabric that won't be competitive or in high demand, no import quotas were ever imposed on it like they have been on cotton and wool. Therefore we could supply a silk shirt at a low price.

PSP: *How did you sell your shirt to the customer?*

Melwani: We advertised it in upscale publications like *Cosmopolitan*, then shipped it from the back of a store in New York City. We had actually bartered to get that space from someone else who was operating a store there. When you don't have money, you're forced to be creative.

PSP: *What was the response to your first shirt ad?*

Melwani: We sold 3,000 shirts. It was a simple product, a basic man-tailored shirt for women from a fairly standard pattern that we designed ourselves.

PSP: *Did subsequent ads pull as well for you?*

Melwani: Oh, no—and we couldn't figure out why not. That first ad had a power of its own. Believe it or not, we even repeated that first ad to see if it would pull as well again. And in the middle of our market testing, another company offered to buy the marketing rights. Since we were undercapitalized, we had to sell it, and then we had to come up with a new business idea.

PSP: *What was your situation then?*

Melwani: We were going absolutely nowhere. We had tried two or three other products, our company was in immense debt, and the one product that had worked for us had now been taken over by someone else. We had become a wholesaler, which was just what I didn't want to be.

PSP: *What was your objection to being a wholesaler?*

Melwani: After I graduated from college, I worked for my uncle who was in the import business. Eventually I wound up in sales management. What I saw was a problem I felt I could change for the better. Our company would purchase something that cost us $1 by the time it got to our warehouse. That item would then be sold to the consumer for $4, $5, and even $6. To me, that margin was incredible. For a product that might easily be sold to the consumer for $2 why *should* it be sold for $6? This was a major obstacle for the salesperson to overcome and I knew that because I was doing the selling.

PSP: *Did you have a marketing strategy for the first silk shirt?*

Melwani: Yes, and it had to be a very careful one. We had to look at absolutely everything. At that time, and because of my previous experience with my uncle's company, I knew quite a lot about marketing. I knew, for instance, that the only way for this shirt to make it was to have about 50 hooks in the marketing campaign. In my mind, the price, written copy, style, color, fabric, and prospective customer all had to be right. When we went to sell the shirt, it was to do it five or six different ways. We couldn't just depend on one single marketing feature.

PSP: *Was there one thing you had to watch out for in particular?*

Melwani: We consciously tried *not* to cheapen the shirt by claiming to be *only* so much. I felt it was important to let the buyer discover that for herself.

PSP: *Why was that?*

Melwani: One of the dangers (and this usually happens with a product known for its high or quality price tag) is that a lower price makes people shy away. For instance, imagine this. Gold is selling for $375 an ounce and I come to you and say, "Here's gold for $200 an ounce." What would be your first reaction?

PSP: *I wouldn't believe it was real gold.*

Melwani: Of course you wouldn't believe it. And this is precisely what we had to overcome. The country was in a recession at that time, with high inflation rates. An inexpensive silk blouse was unlikely to be believed. We could not sell it on just one level. We were fortunate to be in the right place at the right time, with the right vehicle and product and the market for it. Then came problems with the company that had bought our first shirt out.

PSP: *What problems did you have with them?*

Melwani: We had been going nowhere, as I said before, and the one product that had worked for us had been taken over by this other company. When we came out with the second shirt, believe it or not, the other company objected strongly.

PSP: *Why was that?*

Melwani: Fear on their part that it looked similar to the first and the marketing concept was similar.

PSP: *What was different about it?*

Melwani: The styling and the fabrics were different. It really wasn't the same shirt at all. I had left enough room there so as not to confuse the two shirts in the minds of the buyers.

PSP: *How did you handle the other company's objections?*

Melwani: I said, "Look—you're not buying enough of these shirts for us to survive as a company, so I really can't do anything else. But I'll tell you what I will do—if you don't sell as many shirts as you think you will, I'll take them all back." Finally they relented, but it took some doing because they had issued ultimatums.

PSP: *Had they threatened with legal actions?*

Melwani: No—I don't think that would have meant anything in our situation anyway. It was what I call a "workout situation." To me legal actions are just delaying and bullying tactics—they don't really solve anything. If you can talk it out, it always works better. We held some strong cards there and we had to go ahead with the other shirt in order to stay in business. They went on to do very well with their shirt.

PSP: *So you designed a new ad campaign for your new shirt?*

Melwani: Yes, we started all over.

PSP: *Considering all this, did your new ad pull well?*

Melwani: Let me put it this way. It took us from July until the next March to deliver on all the orders we got. We were very pleased. This was the rebirth of our company.

PSP: *Would you say you had finally found the formula that worked for you?*

Melwani: Yes, I would. But at that time, we were only doing print ads. Next, we developed a catalog of silk shirts. For us, a catalog was a piece of cake compared to space advertising.

PSP: *In what ways was it easier?*

Melwani: I had already built a lot of discipline in this area and I knew much more at this time than I had known when I started with ads. In a space ad, your ad is placed against lots of other advertisers, so there's a lower attention span on the part of the reader.

It's much harder to sell to somebody who is not looking for something. That's the difference between a salesperson and an order taker. One is a professional. And our ads were like the professional salesperson who really has to get out there and sell.

PSP: *What's the difference in a catalog?*

Melwani: There you have a totally different environment. You can cluster many items and the customer's attention is only on your products.

PSP: *What was the biggest single sale you ever made?*

Melwani: The biggest sale would have been $200,000.

PSP: *Do you plan to expand into new markets?*

Melwani: We are already expanding into new markets by selling items for men and children, as well as expanding the women's market. We are selling an age-old product that has withstood the test of time. Silk goes back thousands of years. It has proven itself and we feel we can sell it at all levels. I've seen silk wallets, book covers, toys, puppets, and even paintings. We began with that one shirt ad and then added a catalog. We now have four different catalogs. We are opening a 15,000-square-foot store on Fifth Avenue in New York City and we are already online with our viewtron electronic marketing operation. [This store has been joined by a host of others that Royal Silk has since opened around the country. All are reportedly doing well.]

PSP: *Do you get a lot of customer input?*

Melwani: [He chuckles.] We hear all kinds of things. The number one critic of our product is the customer. When a customer says something we have to jump. And we like that. If we didn't monitor that traffic, we wouldn't know what the heck we were doing wrong with our product. That's what a good salesperson monitors. He or she forms the bridge between the company and the customer.

PSP: *How have things changed for you personally since the first successful shirt?*

Melwani: I'm having a lot more fun. I don't have to struggle with small thinking and small personalities any longer. I can try things without worrying if every little thing is going to work out. I have the great privilege now of making mistakes without the insecurity attached to them. I don't have to listen to a chorus of voices whispering in my ear, "What if. . . ."

PSP: *Do you see any difference between selling to Americans and, say, selling to the Japanese?*

Melwani: No. Selling is selling. You do have to learn and understand the culture you're selling to, and then use that as a tool to sell. Culture has to do with perceptions, objects, symbols, and language—whether it's on a tribal level or on a corporate one. That's why I say that to be a good salesperson, you have to know the product. A good salesperson, to me, is not a good talker, or somebody who can sell something quickly—no, the best salesperson is the one who can get the people coming back all the time. I guess it's like the trading my father did. You must identify the buyer and the product, and make the two understand each other, like each other, and want each other.

6

Feasting on Fowl
Lonnie "Bo" Pilgrim

"Selling creates a new frontier, it creates new life . . ."

When Lonnie "Bo" Pilgrim was barely 9 years of age his father suddenly died, leaving Lonnie's mother and her seven children to struggle for themselves. "I had to grow up quickly," he said with a distant look as he contemplated his past. Pilgrim's humble beginnings, and his faith in a higher power that helps us use our innate gifts, have enabled him to build an empire that is rock solid.

I met Pilgrim through a mutual friend and when I toured his extensive and impressive business facilities I was struck by his dedication to every facet of his giant corporation. A practical man, Pilgrim has combined a savvy sense of what the market wants with the creativity to expand his product base by stretching the limits of what can be done with ordinary chicken. In the otherwise pedestrian field of chicken production and distribution, he is a unique figure. Doing a million dollars of business a day is no mean feat.

Pilgrim thrives on such superlative performance. His boneless chicken—that's right, whole chicken sold with the skin on and no bones at all—has broken sales records in the Texas stores that are lucky enough to stock it.

How did he create such a rare bird? By trying thousands of different ways to bone a chicken, by leaving the skin intact, and by doing it in as little time as possible for peak efficiency. Pilgrim took home two chickens a night for months, practiced deboning them in his kitchen, invented special tools for the job, and finally got it down to a science. He then taught his factory workers how to duplicate the performance and, presto, a new product, which created new and expanded markets, was born.

We talked about his early beginnings and the hard work and long hours that have gone into making this incredible success called Pilgrim Industries. The life-size chicken sculpture that sits on his desk may not be as beautiful as a peacock nor as stately as an eagle in flight, but for Bo its homely appearance represents many hard-won battles, often not far removed from scratching in the dirt.

I have always been fascinated by the way that one success

leads to another. Pilgrim's successful venture into the previously untapped market of Mexico to sell eggs would never have come to pass if he hadn't had the courage to try. He might never have tried if he hadn't taken other risks and been successful before. Bo Pilgrim has tried and failed many times. He knows that failure need not be devastating. He has experienced its bite, and he knows that wounds can be healed by trying again and getting it right.

Lonnie "Bo" Pilgrim puts a chicken bone on his plate in the executive dining room at Pilgrim Industries, leans back in his chair and smiles: "We would not be at the top of our industry without our high standards for efficiency. We salvage everything but the squawk." Bo Pilgrim, who started selling before age nine, has turned a small feed store into a major company with an astonishing $1 million a day sales volume from the sale of chicken (1/2 million per day) and table eggs (100,000 dozen per day).

Many of Bo Pilgrim's 2,500 employees have surpassed his high school education with grades, diplomas, and degrees, yet he leads his entire conglomerate based on the simple lessons he has learned in years of self-education and a few specialized seminars. His company's slogan, "Honest Chicken from Real Pilgrims," reflects the deeply ingrained values inherited from his father, who earned the admiration and respect of his community through his high standards of integrity. It is no wonder that Pilgrim Industries has made "integrity" a major pillar of its official marketing philosophy. The company brochure proudly dictates: "Our whole philosophy at Pilgrim is based on never promising more than we can deliver. And delivering everything that we promise. Living up to our commitments—honestly. That's the way we operate." There is much to learn from the way Bo Pilgrim operates. He doesn't mince words. Here is the transcript of our interview—a rare opportunity to trace the successful steps of a superachiever.

PSP: *Your company specializes in selling chicken and eggs. What is your current sales volume?*
Pilgrim: We are producing a half a million chickens a day and

100,000 dozen table eggs. Our volume is about $1 million in sales a day.

PSP: *Do you remember your first sale ever?*

Pilgrim: My father was postmaster and he ran a general merchandise store in a little community. He would tell me that I could earn one soft drink for every five drinks I sold. So I made myself a little cart and went three-fourths of a mile down the road to the cotton gin, which was run by my grandfather. I spent about 30 minutes and sold five drinks for a nickel each. When I got back to the store, I would give my daddy the money and he'd give me my drink. That turned me on to selling. One of my first sales goals in life was to earn enough money to be able to walk up to the drink box and buy a cola anytime I wanted to without having to ask my daddy.

PSP: *When did you reach your first sales goal?*

Pilgrim: Within a couple of years. Before my father died, I was working for him in the summertime hanging potato sacks on a grader. I earned $1 a week, and at the end of the week, I could go to town with someone and buy a chicken fried steak for 35¢ with all the trimmings and spend 15¢ for the show.

PSP: *How old were you when your father died?*

Pilgrim: I was 9 years old when he died on April 11, 1939. There were seven kids in the family, the youngest only six months old. Only one was already married, so things were a little rough. My mother had only $80 in savings. I had to work my way through high school. It was a matter of survival. My mother remarried, but I didn't accept the marriage, so I left home to live with my grandmother.

PSP: *What did your grandmother do?*

Pilgrim: She was a housewife. I remember her dealing with a peddler who visited us with his truck. We raised chickens in the back yard and the peddler would buy them or trade for supplies. He went down the road and sold the chickens to someone else. This created some interest for me.

PSP: *When did you start your own business?*

Pilgrim: My brother and I bought an old feed store back in the mid-1940s. We started out selling horse feed, dairy feed, and chicken feed. In 1950, we built our own feed mill to expand our business. In 1951, I went into the Army and spent two years in California. I noticed that they used a better system for feeding chickens. Back home, we were handling feed in 100-pound bags, by hand; out there, they were conveying feed automatically from a feed tank. When I came home in 1953, I installed a feed tank and tied it in with an automatic feeder regulated by a time clock. We were selling a lot of people on using this new system because they didn't have to be there to feed the chickens.

PSP: *What kinds of goals did you set for your business during this phase?*

Pilgrim: I wanted to do more volume, I wanted to give my customers more value than they could get from our competition, I wanted to give them good, personal service, and at the same time I wanted to make a profit. But the most important item on my list was integrity.

PSP: *Why?*

Pilgrim: My father taught me that by his actions. For ten years after he died, everyone was telling me about his high standards for integrity. Moral values became real important to me early. The disappointment of my father dying led me to join the church and I said to myself and God that if I ever achieved anything, I'd certainly want to recognize Him as being a partner with me in that journey. He didn't go out and part any waters for me, but I've always had this concept that He knows what's going on and He gives us a brain to decide. We have to make decisions and choices throughout our lives.

PSP: *And you became a decision-maker at a very early age.*

Pilgrim: I have always taken a position of leadership. When I was a kid, I would always hold up my hand and ask the others to team up with me as the leader of the group. It didn't make any difference whether we were playing a game or not. It was instinct.

PSP: *I can see that you have a lot of drive and ambition.*

Pilgrim: I always had a lot of drive. I remember when I came back from the Army, my brother told me that he'd like to sell out to me. I asked him why. He said, "Bo, you have so much ambition to be rich, it just drives me up the wall." Luckily, I talked him out of it and I told him that I needed him as my senior partner.

PSP: *Did other people think the same way about you?*

Pilgrim: A friend of mine once told me that some day I'd be worth a million dollars because of my drive.

PSP: *You said earlier that your first financial goal was to be able to buy your own cola. What was your second goal?*

Pilgrim: My second goal was to make a million dollars.

PSP: *When did you reach it?*

Pilgrim: In the early 1960s. After I made my first million dollars, I said, "Maybe I can make 10 million." After I made 10 million, my next goal was to make 10 million a year. I'm proud to say that I've reached all these goals.

PSP: *We talked about your automatic feed system and how it increased sales. What was your next growth step?*

Pilgrim: In the 1950s we started to own the chickens and put them out to the growers. We'd furnish the feed and pay them so much per pound for growing the chickens.

PSP: *How about your competition?*

Pilgrim: When we started out in this area, there were about 20 other companies in the chicken-and-egg business, among them very big firms like Quaker and Ralston-Purina. Now, we're the only ones left who produce chickens in northeast Texas.

PSP: *How did you outsell your competitors?*

Pilgrim: I viewed my competitors as a challenge—I didn't expect them to go away. I had to look for new ideas to beat them in quality, service, and price. I used to say about the quality of our feed, "I won't ship a sack of feed that I can't taste myself." If I lost a customer to Purina, I tried to figure out some way to get that customer back. I worked hard at coming up with better ways to serve each customer's needs. I think the main reason my competitors disappeared is because we were willing to give more for the dollar.

PSP: *How have you been able to build a successful business on such a limited product line?*
Pilgrim: There are two things. First, selling. Selling creates a new frontier, it creates new life. Second, we've built our business on the cost side. We've out-produced others based on cost. My philosophy has been that you'll survive in this industry only if you can maintain your cost level within the top third of the industry. You can't be average in selling and average in cost if you want to survive. I've always preached to my people that we're not performing until we get into the top third.

PSP: *How do you reach the top third?*
Pilgrim: The key lies in having a management control system and having managers who understand those goals and perform in that direction. I attended many American Management Association seminars and designed our own MBO (management by objectives) system. I also set up a monthly award system where we compare actual performance versus goals. If my managers meet the goals, they'll receive a bonus check at the end of the month.

PSP: *What other factors have contributed to your reaching the top?*
Pilgrim: We diversified. We began to own our distribution network. We built our own rendering plant, we began to control the breeder farms, then we raised laying hens and sold table eggs. My goal was to have an integrated operation, I always wanted to do the whole thing—play every golf ball on the course. We went into the trucking business, since we thought that we could operate our own trucks more efficiently. We bought a Chevrolet dealership, and in 1969 I bought a bank to handle some of our money needs. I always thought that I could do for myself just as well and as economically as someone else on the outside could do for me.

PSP: *Do you consider yourself a good salesperson?*
Pilgrim: I guess it's just been second nature to me. You have to be able to sell your ideas to reach the top.

PSP: *What are the qualities of a good salesperson?*

Pilgrim: First, you have to understand people and their per-sonalities. Second, you ought to understand what they need to buy, rather than what you want them to have. Third, you need to project to them that you can win their respect if given an opportunity. Don't ask for things up front, but ask for an opportunity.

PSP: *What was your biggest sale ever?*

Pilgrim: In 1981, I went to Mexico to look at chicken opera-tions and talked to various government officials about their needs for table eggs. I left with an order for 750 truckloads of eggs to be delivered to Mexico City in 90 days. No one had ever attempted to deliver $12 million worth of eggs to Mexico City before. I sold these eggs on an open account and we did everything we told them we would do plus extra. They paid promptly and we made an additional sale the following year. I treated them just like customers in Dallas or L.A.

PSP: *What's your measure of success?*

Pilgrim: My measure of success is based upon the results I can produce. Results are the product of ability plus experience times motivation. It's not necessarily measured in dollars.

PSP: *Why not?*

Pilgrim: Money was never my number one priority. I always looked at that as a by-product. I think someone who is driven by money becomes like H. L. Hunt, who brings his lunch in a brown sack. I always told myself, "I don't eat lunch out of a brown sack—I'd rather eat lunch at the Country Club." If money is going to be your driving force, you are going to become very conservative and try to hoard money. To me, money is something you use to make things happen. You can use it to build a business, to help others, or to give it to the preacher. I am not interested in storing money.

PSP: *You are currently introducing a very innovative and almost revolutionary product, the boneless chicken. How did you come up with this idea?*

Pilgrim: About three years ago, we had a slowdown in sales and I tried to find new ways to increase demand. I looked at how other countries sold chicken and found that 65 percent of all chickens sold in Japan were sold boneless. I searched for instructions to learn how to debone a chicken without cutting the skin or cutting the chicken in half. I started calling experts from all over the country, and began to examine the existing methods for deboning chickens. Every evening, I took two chickens home with me to practice deboning until I could do it in less than 20 minutes. With help from people in our plant, we created special workbenches and tools to speed up the process even more. We can now debone a chicken without cutting the skin and leaving all the meat in its original position, in about six minutes. We named it Bo Pilgrim's Boneless Miracle. We have applied for a patent for this new deboning process.

PSP: *How many people do you employ?*

Pilgrim: About 2,500.

PSP: *Would you agree that a company is not as much influenced by the management in place as by the personality of its leader?*

Pilgrim: I think that the personality of the chief executive certainly sets the tone for what is expected of employees.

PSP: *What is it that you expect of yourself?*

Pilgrim: Business is like a game to me. I have a friend who plays golf every day. He is constantly trying to improve his score—so am I. Business is an extremely competitive game and you can't daydream or assume that something is going to happen—you have to make it happen. If you lose, you just start preparing for the next game. Don't worry about the game you lost, it's the next one coming up that you prepare for. You have to stay in the top third to be recognized and to survive.

PSP: *So it appears that success begins by having high expectations of yourself.*

Pilgrim: Yes. I had a guy once who quit on me and I asked him why. He said that I expected so much. I talked to him only once a week, but he perceived my expectations.

PSP: *How do you deal with adversity?*

Pilgrim: I just accept it as a fact of life, it's inevitable. You can't change adversity. I devote my time and interest to those things that I can change.

PSP: *You are a positive thinker.*

Pilgrim: Of course. I think it goes back to my childhood, when my father died . . . it was a matter of survival.

PSP: *When you were 9 years old, did you have a vision of what you were going to do at age 54?*

Pilgrim: I had a vision of being successful; however, not to this extent. I guess you could say that I have exceeded my dreams by far.

PSP: *What would you do differently, if you had to start all over again?*

Pilgrim: Obviously, education is more important today than when I started. I was an entrepreneur before I got out of high school. I would get a college education now if I had to do it over again.

PSP: *It sounds like you learned more out of necessity. What would you consider the key lessons that you've learned?*

Pilgrim: First, you have to develop a high level of discipline and apply it to your personal, spiritual and professional life. Just as the Bible has the Ten Commandments to follow, there are certain principles that apply to any business, like planning, organizing, motivating, problem solving, appraising performance, and so on. You can't just understand these principles from a textbook point of view. You have to go a step further and apply them consistently. There are many people who learn the basic principles and recite them, but don't practice them.

PSP: *How do you go about translating this knowledge into action skills?*

Pilgrim: We developed an ongoing, everyday system, so people can see it and become part of it. We select our people very carefully. We don't take long shots; we train them thoroughly, we give them an extensive orientation so each one understands the purpose of his or her job, responsibility and authority. We agree on goals and we measure them. So there is no one in our organization running around wondering what they are supposed to be doing.

PSP: *And you set the example.*

Pilgrim: Yes. I don't ever ask a person to do anything that I am not willing to do myself. I think you can have all the company goals you want, but if a person doesn't get job satisfaction, you can forget it. You need to achieve job satisfaction and personal satisfaction or you're not motivated.

PSP: *What do you feel are the key motivating factors for your sales force?*

Pilgrim: The two motivators in achieving our sales goals are monetary rewards and personal pride. I am proud of their ability to achieve results, they participate in the goal-setting process, and they are well rewarded for their achievements.

PSP: *How many hours do you work a day?*

Pilgrim: I get up at 5:30 A.M. and I go to bed at 10 P.M. Most of the time, I am doing something that contributes to the business. I don't believe a successful business can be managed on 40 hours a week. If a manager is not working 60 hours a week, he's not doing his job. I tease my senior VPs with the saying, "Anything after 20 hours a day is free time."

PSP: *You're married and you've raised three children.*

Pilgrim: We've been married nearly 30 years and we have had less than six heated arguments and no walkouts.

PSP: *When you look at your family and compare raising three children with raising a company employing 2,500 people and reaching sales of $1 million a day, which do you consider the greater success?*

Pilgrim: I wouldn't consider myself successful if I had gained the whole world and failed my family

PSP: *How would you like to be remembered?*

Pilgrim: I'd like to be remembered as a good father, as a religious person, and as an outstanding businessman of integrity.

7

Everyone's Cup of Tea

Mo Siegel

"There is a part of me that clearly wants to make money, big money, and fairly fast. This part of me is motivated by achievment and ambition. The other part of me is altruistic; the need to do good."

We were very excited about our trip to visit Mo Siegel at Celestial Seasonings' headquarters in Boulder, Colorado, having already heard bits and pieces of the phenomenal story of this flower-child-turned-entrepreneur. (That story was made all the more remarkable by the purchase of Siegel's company later that year by corporate giant Kraft Foods.) Any doubts we may have harbored about the success of the transition from herb-collecting hippie to president of a $30 million company were immediately swept away when we were led into Mo Siegel's attractively appointed private office—despite the fact that we walked past his ten-speed bike resting against the reception room wall.

Mo Siegel is an enthusiastic purveyor of healthy products. One senses his excitement by the way he sips tea (as if he's tasting fine wine), by the rise in his voice when he describes the challenges of his business, and by his entire company's dedication to providing the best possible product and service for the consumer. But Mo is more than a one-dimensional picture of a business tycoon out to make a buck. In him we found the best qualities of our young culture. Mo Siegel respects sound business principles and wants to make a profit, but he also wants to make a worthwhile contribution to the society that supports his work.

Perhaps it is this very combination that helped Siegel to weather the early struggles. In our interview, he describes how one crop failure almost ruined his business, and he goes on to talk about the lessons he learned from this experience. He didn't let that setback deter him from his ultimate goals, and he looks back to that time with a kind of reverence. In Mo's mind, the greatest affliction in life is never to have been afflicted. Said another way, we need afflictions to test and challenge us. Without them, we would have no measure of our own abilities—of our own creativity.

Siegel is an avid skier and cyclist, riding his bike to work and back home every day. He believes that wealth means little without health, and that when an organization can attach itself to something greater than itself—to an overall concept of doing good for others—we will all profit.

This is a truly American rags-to-riches story about a boy with a dream, the man he became, and the success he built. He did it all on his own—took the risk, borrowed the money, developed the concept, and worked very hard until it became the reality he always knew it would. Mo Siegel's super success is a shining example of the opportunity that is open to anyone who looks for it.

With only a high school education and a dream to make his first million dollars by his 25th birthday, Mo Siegel started Celestial Seasonings in 1971. He was 20 then. Today, at 33, his sales are approaching $30 million annually and he is confidently expecting to reach the $100 million mark by 1990—without giving up the unique values and principles described in this exclusive interview with PSP.

PSP: *You made your first million dollars at age 26. How do you explain that?*
Siegel: I had an objective since about the age of six that by the age of 25, I would have made my first million. I think it was the first week after I turned 26 that I reached it on paper.
PSP: *How old were you when you started Celestial Seasonings?*
Siegel: I was 20.
PSP: *When you started, what kind of goals or dreams did you pursue?*
Siegel: From the very beginning, I would tell bankers, "I am out to build a $100 million company, and I am going to start with selling herb tea." They thought I had lost my mind.
PSP: *What made you decide to enter the herb tea business?*
Siegel: Part of me wanted to go into an art-oriented field like the movies or greeting cards and another part of me was very

health driven. I knew as a child that I was going to be in business and I've always had an inclination from a very young age for being philosophical. I finally decided that I could be much more useful as a person by being dedicated to health.

PSP: *It seems like you had a good understanding of that market.*

Siegel: I think I am fairly strategic when I look at a business. I saw the health opportunity very early. I looked at the European tea market and noticed that herb teas sold well, but Americans hadn't started to use them yet. I saw that more and more people were getting interested in health. They began to exercise, they took vitamins, and they became more health conscious.

PSP: *When you started Celestial Seasonings back in 1971, how did the people feel about herb teas?*

Siegel: When I started, people still thought that herb teas were weird. In the consumer's mind, herb tea didn't taste very good and you only drank it when you were sick. I wanted to make herb tea that tasted good and sell people on drinking it all the time.

PSP: *You must have faced a number of challenges.*

Siegel: I remember when I went with my gunnysack collecting herbs in the mountains, many thought of me as an odd guy. But that's the price you pay when you introduce a new idea. Dr. Ken Cooper, the father of aerobics, told me once that when he went to Dallas to promote his fitness program, they thought he had lost his marbles. When I was out picking tea, I was the butt of countless Euell Gibbons jokes.

PSP: *They thought you were a health nut?*

Siegel: No, I was a fanatic then; I am a health nut now.

PSP: *You have mellowed.*

Siegel: Yes. In fact, I jokingly say these days that the reason I exercise, take my vitamins, eat my alfalfa sprouts, and drink my herb tea is for one simple reason: to be able to eat as much ice cream as I want.

PSP: *How did you sell your herb teas back when you started?*

Siegel: I made cold calls on health food stores in my old Datsun. I love selling. I feel that I am doing something good for other people just by selling our product.

PSP: *But you are not only motivated by being good to other people?*

Siegel: There is a battle that I go through sometimes. There is a part of me that clearly wants to make money, big money, and fairly fast. This part of me is motivated by achievement and ambition. The other part is altruistic; the need to do good.

PSP: *What would you consider to be the best approach in selling?*

Siegel: I think it's not hard to sell if you are benefit oriented. I believe that nobody buys anything if there is not a benefit. I always say to our people, "If you can't give your customer a WIFM—the *what's in it for me*—don't show up." To make your sales calls meaningful, there should be a specific reason for the call besides the WIFM. Like something new, something different. I also have a rule in selling, that you should always make a friend.

PSP: *Build relationships.*

Siegel: Yes. Make a friend, because if you don't get the sale, at least you've got a friend. Be close to your customers, care about them, service their needs.

PSP: *To what do you attribute your success?*

Siegel: I think that either you follow the basic principles or you get nailed. There are some rules that work almost all the time. If you don't set goals, you don't get anywhere. That's so basic. The thing that I enjoy in my business is figuring out the overall mission, then establishing goals and developing the strategies, the action plans, and the calendar by which they must be completed. Another basic principle would be to be persistent in your work. To work smarter. Follow your priorities. Do number one, two, and three first in the day. I go as far as putting time percentages next to the tasks. For example, I may decide to invest 40 percent of the working day in priority number one. At the end of the day I score how I've done for the day.

PSP: *So you know how well you've performed.*

Siegel: I do the same with our business. I use the computer to measure our performance and compare it to that of other businesses. We are members of the Strategic Planning Institute. According to their data, we rank in the upper 98 percent for productivity of all 2,000 companies that have been plugged into that model.

PSP: *Let's go back to your initial goal to build a $100 million company. Where are you today?*

Siegel: We're approaching $30 million.

PSP: *You said in a recent interview that you expect to reach $100 million by 1990.*

Siegel: We are working on it.

PSP: *What was your first major obstacle after you got your business started? Your first doubt that you'd ever reach your goals?*

Siegel: I never thought that. Never. But we sure had a lot of obstacles . . . although I finally concluded that the greatest affliction in life is never to have been afflicted. I give talks every so often on what I call the ten principles of success. One of them is the acceptance of failure and persistence toward success. If you use a clear set of goals, you will reach about 85 percent of them and 15 percent will be disappointments.

PSP: *How about your first major disappointment?*

Siegel: Well, we once contracted a peppermint crop in Wisconsin because we were dissatisfied with our European imports. We bought the field standing and it rained for two weeks in August. Then a frost hit and we lost most of the crop. We almost went broke. That was our first major business failure. Nobody enjoys failing, but we can learn from what we do wrong and in the process we find out how to get better.

PSP: *You use lemons to make lemonade.*

Siegel: There are a lot of people who don't understand this principle. When they fail, they give up and seek shelter. For example, we worked over two years on developing a chamomile shampoo. We went through seven chemists to get the product that we wanted. We could have given up, but we persisted and asked: "What did we learn from the last failure? How can we do better?"

PSP: *What quality standards were you trying to reach?*

Siegel: Very simple. We said that we wouldn't market our new product unless we could beat our competition in a blind test.

PSP: *Speaking of competition. Not too long ago you cancelled a fully developed advertising campaign that compared your new tea against Lipton's. According to a* New York Times *article, the tests showed that you could beat competition in the blind tests, but you decided against the entire campaign.*

Siegel: Yes. Our ad agency and our marketing people had all the research and said it was the right thing to do. It was very tempting because our key competitor sells black tea. That's a $900 million market. The herb tea market is only about $90 million. So there was an element of greed. It took a lot of soul searching to clarify what our real values were. Finally, I decided that I did not want to make a fortune by bad mouthing anybody. There were so many good things about our products we could say. I could not take it any longer and cancelled the program. I realized that it was a very good decision, one that led me to grow further.

PSP: *It made you question your values.*

Siegel: Yes. I see that competitive pressures bring more and more challenges to basic values. There are very simple reasons for this. The gross national product in the decade of the 1970s grew only about 1.7 percent in real dollars. From the best projections I have seen, the growth in the decade of the 1980s will be even lower, about 1.3 percent. These trends show that we are dealing with a basically flat economy. All we are doing is changing and reshuffling. In our business, we are trying to change the market from coffee and black tea to herb tea. The pressure on business giants is growing and the competitive nature of American business is increasing rapidly. I think that things will get very odd for a while until we learn how to be a little more cooperative.

PSP: *How do you react when a competitor like Lipton's*

introduces a new line of herb teas? I see you as fairly competitive. . . .

Siegel: I can't stand it and I won't stop improving ours until we beat them. You're right, I am competitive. But I am only concerned with two areas: customer and product. I ask, "Is the customer happy?" and, "Are we making the best product?" That's all I care about.

PSP: *So instead of attacking the competition, you focus your energies on serving your customers better.*

Siegel: Absolutely.

PSP: *What is it that you like most about your business?*

Siegel: I want to establish a value system in our organization so that if I got hit on my bike someday, the value system would stay and the company would do well based on these values.

PSP: *What components would you include in this system?*

Siegel: We've already developed a very detailed belief statement. You could compare it to four legs on a stool. The first leg is our love of our product. We are a product-driven company, we want to develop the best products. We are improving three of our four top sellers this year. Improving—and they weren't bad. People around here often ask, "If it isn't broken—why fix it?" To me, it doesn't count how good our products are, but how good they can be. We constantly test our teas with thousands of people a year. We will not let anyone make a better cup of tea.

PSP: *What's your second leg?*

Siegel: Our love of our customers and consumers. Our customers are the distributors. The consumer is the end user. We feel that if we can't sell benefits to the consumer, we shouldn't be in the business. We love to fill consumers' needs and benefit people. We are getting over 200 letters from consumers per week telling us that we're on the right track.

PSP: *If you don't serve a need, you won't be needed.*

Siegel: If you're not filling needs, then you're tricking people. I'd rather die broke and be useful than make all the money in the world selling useless things. Our third leg is love of art and beauty. For example, we've just developed this new package for restaurants and it's probably the most beautiful tea package anybody has ever done. Four-color artwork on each packet. We use some of the best artists in the world for our packaging. The fourth leg is based on the dignity of the individual. If you develop work systems that dignify work and dignify individuals, life will certainly become more pleasant and also more productive. I guess some of my biggest disappointments have been in this area during my years as an entrepreneur. I've learned since that, as a manager, you should rise on people's shoulders, not around their necks.

PSP: *You don't have a business school education.*

Siegel: No, I have only a high school education, but I think that if you want to have a good life, you have to learn from birth to the grave. One of my ten rules of success is that you've got to learn and grow. I won't ride my bike to work without listening to educational tapes. I read all the time, I take classes, I just got into the Young Presidents Organization.

PSP: *What tapes do you listen to?*

Siegel: I love Dr. Norman Vincent Peale. I have over 30 of his cassettes. I enjoy Peter Drucker, and Newstrack, an executive cassette service.

PSP: *The best education is an open mind.*

Siegel: Yes, and to be able to use other people's minds. I have many heroes who have inspired me to grow in my business. For example, next week I will send out postcards to some 1,500 customers thanking them for their efforts. I hope by this summer I will have 10,000 customers on my postcard mailing list. I thought of it after I read Joe Girard and Mary Kay.

PSP: *Your employees receive a great deal of training.*

Siegel: Yes, I want my managers to have at least 30 hours of training per year. Salespeople should probably have more. I keep suggesting that they all have cassette players in their cars, so that when they are stuck in traffic they are getting smart.

PSP: *You developed a comprehensive value system for your company. How about your values as a person?*

Siegel: I think the greatest danger a person can have in his or her life is to become "I-important." The greatest satisfaction a person can have is to become selfless. People who give are the happiest people in the world, not the people who take.

PSP: *How would money fit into this philosophy?*

Siegel: I had this thought about my own values and I pictured that I had died and gone to heaven. The ancients of days pulled out the record books and they asked what I had done with my life. I said that I made a lot of money. They thumbed through the books and said that they didn't see that. I said that I had sold more herb teas than anybody else, but they couldn't see that either. Then I said that I had dedicated my life to making people healthy, I had dedicated my life to being a true friend to people, a giving person, I had dedicated my life to my family, and they said that they saw that. When I went through this experience, I realized that you should check your values very carefully and do what is worthwhile to the world and not just worthwhile to you. A selfish life is a life not worth having.

PSP: *Meaning comes before money.*

Siegel: I think so.

PSP: *What's your definition of success?*

Siegel: As a corporation, measure it in sales, profits, and dignity of the individual. As a person, of all the greatest human achievements, the raising of a good family is the greatest achievement. You could build any size corporation imaginable and it would not equal the success of raising good children. That's the highest task a person could do in life.

PSP: *You have been raised by an older sister?*

Siegel: Yes, my mother died when I was 2 years old.

PSP: *How large was your family?*

Siegel: Four kids; two older sisters and one younger sister.

PSP: *What did your father do?*

Siegel: He owned a kind of discount department store. He was an auctioneer. He did pretty well. He was a real driver. He worked like crazy all the time. He always thought that I was lazy. I do like to say that I never got one penny from him to build Celestial Seasonings.

PSP: *You had a tough childhood.*

Siegel: I think I did. My father was such a driver. He was very hard for me to get along with. He had his set of views of the world. Anything that was different from those was not tolerated.

PSP: *He sounds like a father I know.*

Siegel: At the age of 17, there was no further financial aid or anything else, because my father and I had such diametric opposite views of religion. I ended up having a deep Christian faith while he's Jewish.

PSP: *You dealt with a number of big disappointments and had to grow up very fast.*

Siegel: Yes. I have a painting of Abraham Lincoln in my office. He probably had about as many disappointments as anybody. But I believe that the disappointments hardest to bear are those that never come. It's never as bad as you anticipate it to be. I have always believed that you have to accept disappointments and failures in life. It's just part of the formula if you want to succeed. You've got to understand it and work with it.

PSP: *How did you learn to accept disappointments?*

Siegel: I am basically religious. My views are very similar to Dr. Peale's. The foundation of his faith is not in materialism, it's not faith in people, but faith in God. I believe that people become greater by being more God-like rather than by becoming themselves. I don't believe that the self is everything or that by fulfilling yourself you can be this great individual.

PSP: *How would you apply this faith to the reality of business?*

Siegel: Well, take IBM as an example. Thomas Watson, Sr., said, "We will serve our customers better than any other corporation in the world." He made a philosophical statement that rallied the troops. He didn't say we are going to do really well and get rich. Or, it's going to be fun and you are all going to drive great cars. The point is, when an organization of people can attach themselves to something greater than themselves, the greater good comes of it. They perform much better, they go the extra mile because it's more fulfilling, and they are happier.

PSP: *It sets up a new perspective. You won't grow taller if you become the measure of all things. Are you saying that Abraham Maslow's theory of self-actualization is not necessarily motivating?*
Siegel: I do like Maslow. What we need to learn is to balance ego-driven motivation and service motivation. When Watson said that he wanted to service his customers better, he revealed a lot of human ambition. He was able to reconcile his strong ambition to succeed with the desire to do something useful and valuable for other people. My goal is to achieve a balance between the two conflicting forces—a balance in which the giving is the greater force.

Celestial Seasonings' Wisdom . . .

The *Lemon Mist* package tells the story:
    In Texas, years ago, almost all of the oil came from surface operations. Then someone got the idea that there were greater sources of supply deeper down. A well was drilled five thousand feet deep. The result? A gusher. Too many of us operate on the surface. We never go deep enough to find supernatural resources. The result is, we never operate at our best. More time and investment is involved to "go deep" but a gusher will pay off.

—Alfred Armand Montapert
The Supreme Philosophy of Man

The *Chamomile* package quotes:
    Wrinkles should merely indicate where smiles have been.
—Mark Twain

A *Sleepytime* package advises:
    You cannot bring about prosperity by discouraging thrift. You cannot strengthen the weak by weakening the strong. You cannot help the wage earner by pulling down the wage payer.

You cannot further the brotherhood of man by encouraging class hatred. You cannot keep out of trouble by spending more than you earn. You cannot build character and courage by taking away man's initiative and independence. You cannot help men permanently by doing for them what they could and should do for themselves.

—Abraham Lincoln

A *Mandarin Orange Spice* package warns:

The wrongdoer is more unfortunate than the man wronged.

—Democritus

. . . Draws a Steady Flow of Responses

"Please write, we like to respond," urges the lid of each Celestial Seasonings tea box. A flood of 200 letters pours in every week from pleased and happy herb tea lovers.

We selected one letter that seems to reflect best the magic of Mo's Sleepytime tea:

"I was introduced to your tea by my best friend at college. I was a freshman and, not accustomed to the work load, frequently had to stay up very late. When I did, my friend gave me Red Zinger to help keep me alert and happy. As time went on, I got better at budgeting my time, so I got to bed at a more reasonable hour. Then my friend suggested that we close each day with a cup of Sleepytime and a chat about our day— which we did for three years. I grew to cherish the opportunity to sit down with her and have my tea, because it was a way for us to express our friendship.

Time passed, and my friend and I moved to different places. I became engaged to a medical student, and after he got his degree we were married on December 11, 1982. My best friend was one of my bridesmaids, and for a wedding gift she gave us 10 boxes of Sleepytime tea. I cried when I saw it, because I realized that she was encouraging me to continue our tradition of tea and a talk at bedtime. She told me that because of my husband's career she knew we might not have enough time to really talk to each other every day. She gave us the tea to help us communicate, just as she and I had done six years ago when I started college. So now, every night before we go to bed, Michael and I have a cup of tea and a talk. I'm quite sure that our marriage is and will be stronger for this! Too many relationships split up these days because people lose the ability to genuinely communicate—but I believe our 'tea and a talk' policy is one way of insuring a happy marriage.

Thanks again for a wonderful product!"

8

The Highest Form of Persuasion

Barbara Proctor

"Whatever you plant or leave behind flowers into something you will see again."

Interviewing Barbara Proctor is not easy. She is a demanding woman who has little time for self-indulgence and less for self-pity. She has spent a lifetime working her way up and, by her own admission, everything has been a piece of cake since she got an education. Proctor started life in the most inauspicious of circumstances. Dirt poor, black in the still-segregated South, she was born to an unwed teenage mother. Her story is now well known and she tells it frequently, more to provide a positive role model for other women than for any other motive.

To say that Barbara Proctor is a feminist would be understating her appeal and her goals. She has said she would like to be a Supreme Court justice one day, and she is, in fact, a law student working toward that goal. Her advertising company, whose rocky beginning she overcame with typical determination and persistence, continues to thrive under the guidance of her son, who Proctor feels has been the greatest blessing in her life of achievement and success.

Proctor is a woman who knows how to talk to anyone and she proved that when she had to go out to sell herself as the owner of her own advertising agency. To say that it was an uphill sell would be the greatest of understatements. She knew she could do a good job for her clients. She carried herself with pride and confidence, knowing these attitudes would be felt by others and would eventually land her the business she knew was out there.

What I have learned from Barbara Proctor can be summed up in one short piece of advice from her: "Take a risk." Women especially, according to Proctor, fear risk. They want guarantees, she says. It is a positive attitude toward taking risks, documented throughout all the interviews in this book, that has allowed Barbara Proctor to succeed and flourish.

I find myself looking forward to Barbara Proctor's future, for in it is a little of my own. She undoubtedly will climb the mountains she is currently measuring. In her ascent there is a step for us all. Our society has made room for the women of courage and determination to take an active role in the future, and women like Proctor are surprising us with their creativity and their boundless energy.

The determination to succeed creates that energy. It frees the mind and the soul. It lets us see clearly all the nuances of choice. Proctor walks with a firm step on ground made solid by enterprising and intelligent assessments of her own potential for growth and her own knowledge of what she has to offer. She knows there is much to be done, and many ways to have an impact on her society. For her, nothing short of the very best will do. That will make life a little better for us all.

"My grandmother always thought I would do something with my life," says Barbara Proctor, founder of Proctor & Gardner Advertising. Ms. Proctor's grandmother was so right.

Born to a 16-year-old unwed mother in the rural mountains of North Carolina, Ms. Proctor's memories of those early days still evoke sights, sounds, and smells. She remembers "the three-room shanty where I attended school . . . hog killing time in the fall . . . and 'feeling' the storm from the mountains days before it arrived." She also remembers segregation and discrimination.

It was Barbara's grandmother who had the most lasting influence on her life. "She taught me that what is important is not on the outside, but inside. She said it is important to put something inside you, some courage, knowledge, or a skill—things that no one can take away," says the chief executive. Her grandmother used to say of her, "She ain't cute, but she's right smart, and one day she's going to amount to something."

Barbara Proctor left the mountains of North Carolina to attend Talladega College in Alabama. She intended to become a teacher. After finishing her undergraduate work in a brief three years, she added another year of psychology and sociology. A summer job at a camp in Michigan earned her enough money to get to Chicago, where she spent every penny. Intending to earn just enough to return to Black Mountain, North Carolina, Barbara took a job writing the copy for record album covers. She's been a resident of the Windy City ever since.

Ms. Proctor's rise in the business world was steady. She grew like an oak tree planted in the sun. She spread her branches with each new spring. And she weathered many storms and cold winter nights. She met the kind of discrimination that black people have faced for centuries and she met a new form of arrogance. Of this experience she says, "In advertising, the only thing worse than being a woman, was being an old woman. I was over 30, female, and black. I had so many things wrong with me that it would have taken all day to figure out which one to blame for my rejections. So I decided not to spend any time worrying about it.

Ms. Proctor started her own advertising agency on $80,000 borrowed from the Small Business Administration. In order to secure the loan, and since she had no collateral, she went to three ad agencies and got job offers of $65,000, $80,000, and $110,000. She used the second as collateral—what she herself was worth on the open market.

The first account was hard to land. It took six months and much selling. "In every case where something would have been an obstacle. I've found a way to turn it to an advantage," says Barbara Proctor. "I say, if you decide you're a winner, then you are. If you decide you're a loser, you're right. I cannot buy the concept that anyone outside is responsible," she explains. Now, more than a decade later, her successful company is worth over $8 million and employs nearly 30 people.

Ethics play an important role in Proctor's business life. "Advertising is the highest form of persuasion," she claims. Believing that advertising can be an instrument for social change, Barbara Proctor turns down accounts that conflict with her notion of social responsibility. "We mold opinions," she states, "therefore we have a responsibility to those people whose opinions we influence." Her company does not advertise alcoholic beverages or cigarettes. She has likewise turned down accounts that she feels are detrimental to the self-esteem of women or blacks. "My belief in the product is unimportant," Proctor muses. "What I resist is the business opportunity to sell questionable or stereotypical products to consumers, especially when there is evidence the product is detrimental or reinforces negative stereotypes."

Barbara Proctor has a "special kind of compassion for the women's movement." She gives advice to women who have not had the courage she has shown by saying, "Women fear risk. They want guarantees. If you are able to risk, able to lose, then you will gain. When women get to the point where they take the risk, fail, and try again, without any loss of self esteem, they will be free."

This incredibly energetic entrepreneur sleeps only two to four hours a day. When asked if she ever gets tired of the hard work and the pushing, she answered, "Of course I do. I feel exploited at times. I feel overworked, misunderstood, misused. . . . All the negatives. My solution is to push those feelings to absurdity. When I realize how absurd it is, and have a great laugh, the feelings are over for another year or so. I never go back and I seldom look back. I've made my share of mistakes and I've learned from them. Energy spent living in the past diminishes your time now and in the future."

PSP: *Ms. Proctor, your ethical views in relation to advertising are well known. How do they differ from the business ethics of your competitors?*

Proctor: I do not presume to judge anyone's standards but my own. I do believe in the "root and fruit" chain of conduct. Whatever you plant or leave behind flowers into something you will see again. You profit or lose by those recurring encounters. So I try to live and utilize my resources in a positive manner.

PSP: *Are you always pleased with your "root and fruit" chain?*

Proctor: When I meet the fruits of my behavior, generally, I am well pleased. Occasionally I have lost revenue because there are some businesses I cannot represent and some people I cannot be comfortable serving. Some business people can separate personal values from business accommodations. I am less complicated and more consistent. There are certain values that remain rock solid with me.

PSP: *Why has your particular philosophy worked so well for you?*

Proctor: Assuming it has—if you mean by that, why do I seem to be more out front than my meager beginning would suggest—I can only express gratitude for that meager beginning. It liberated me in a way that being born in more favored circumstances couldn't have done.

PSP: *In what way was your "meager" beginning liberating?*

Proctor: I have been poorer, uglier, lonelier, more scared than most women . . . and I survived that childhood. Life has been a piece of cake since I got an education. I have enjoyed the freedom that comes only from knowing what's on the other side. I also know that when we buy inclusion and acceptance with conformity, the price bankrupts us spiritually. My greatest wealth is not financial. It is peace of mind. That shows. And it is infectious.

PSP: *Is selling different today from what it was 10 or 15 years ago?*

Proctor: Selling is not different today. It remains the art and skill of exchanging goods and services for something of negotiated value. What *has* changed is the marketplace and the attitude of the buyers.

PSP: *What has changed in the marketplace, in your opinion?*

Proctor: With the development of high technology, specifically television, the buyer is seeing more things, more lifestyles, more options. This places a greater burden on the seller. Not only must a need be generated in order to sell the product, but the buyer must be reinforced in the purchase and conditioned to remain loyal to the choice in the face of newer and more provocative persuasion to make a different decision.

PSP: *Why do people buy?*

Proctor: There are many articulated reasons why people buy: They want something; they need something; a product makes a chore easier; a product makes them more attractive. The basic reason why people buy is the personal gratification they enjoy by successfully negotiating a solution to a perceived problem.

PSP: *Then why do buyers change their minds when it comes time to repurchase?*

Proctor: For the same reason that they bought in the first place. Often they are disappointed with their purchase because the solution requires an internal adjustment. The external purchase alone does not relieve the problem. This does not suggest that the articulated reasons for buying were entirely superficial. Soap is needed to wash clothes clean. The decision-making that goes into brand selection, however, reflects the negotiated choice.

PSP: *In America today are we selling needs or wants?*

Proctor: What we are doing, in many cases, is worse than selling needs, we are generating needs. Women are often the victim of this process. Women are perceived as the turnkey of the American economy. We have commercials and programs blaming women for everything from dirty shirt collars to kids' cavities. If everything in a house is there because a woman bought it or contributed to the purchasing decision, then this attack on women is not sexist, per se. One by-product of men setting up households, which they run alone, and women waiting until later to marry, is that one-person households are the fastest-growing household segment. Now men, too, will have their self-esteem tied to plates they can see their face in and shiny floors.

PSP: *What do you see in the future for working women?*

Proctor: Working women are a permanent factor in the American labor force. Not only are they here to stay in the lower "pink ghettos" of labor, but they have been in the line positions for more than five years now and should begin moving into the upper-management levels of industry and the professions.

PSP: *What do you think awaits them there?*

Proctor: If men are objective enough to allow them access, fine, they will be rewarded. If they continue to reject women in top management, more and more women will simply walk away and begin their own businesses. Women-owned business is the fastest growing segment of all business. Never mind that our little businesses gross, on average, less than $100,000 annually. These women are getting experience and they are shaking the shackles off their minds. The women starting up and struggling today will soon be joined by their better-trained, better-funded, and more-liberated sisters. This will be an exciting decade.

PSP: *How do you think family life will change?*

Proctor: Family patterns have already changed. The new morality has made it socially acceptable for men to walk away from their families. There is a very dangerous economic spectrum looming ahead for women who are stuck in the 1950s' mind-set.

PSP: *What is that?*

Proctor: It is projected that by the year 2000 all of America's poor will be women and children living with women. It's called the feminization of poverty and it's very real.

PSP: *Do you see a way of dealing with these changes?*

Proctor: Yes, I do. The family will have to divide up responsibilities more equitably. An entire wave of "liberated" women have determined that superwoman is dead. They simply cannot be all things to all people. The guilt is diminishing daily, and they have determined that goals and responsibilities are joint commitments by all members of a family. This need not lead to conflict between career women and homemakers. It should lead to a quantification of the home career and stronger protections for the homemaker.

PSP: *How have women in the business world changed companies?*

Proctor: As far as the big picture goes, women haven't changed much of anything. We are still less than 3 percent of the corporate boards of the industrials, and well under 10 percent of top management of top companies overall. And that's where the decision-making occurs. On another level, women have made substantive changes in the business ethics, conduct, and philosophy of the companies they work for.

PSP: *What are your future goals?*

Proctor: The two most immediate are attending law school and building my company into the organization I know it can be. That includes being a sound launching base for the second-generation staffers and officers who helped build this company.

PSP: *What was the biggest sale you ever made?*

Proctor: In 1962 I was an international director for Vee Jay Records in Chicago. While negotiating deals in London, I signed the recording contracts for Vee Jay president E. G. Abner and brought back to America the very first Beatles recording. It amounted to millions of dollars directly and changed American music forever.

PSP: *What was the most important sale for you personally?*

Proctor: After six months of rejection, after rejection from potential clients who had loved me when I was working for someone else but didn't believe a black woman "had it," I landed my first advertising contract with Jewel Foods in Chicago. That was in 1970.

PSP: *To you, what makes a successful salesperson?*

Proctor: The ability to match your product or service with the needs of the buyer. A successful salesperson must look beyond the resistance. He or she must hear beyond the objections being raised; the successful salesperson must penetrate the wall of withdrawal and touch the buyer where he/she is most in need.

PSP: *Where do you feel salespeople most often fail?*

Proctor: Too many salespeople attempt to emphasize the quality of the product rather than how it fits into the quality of the buyer's life. They attempt to wear down resistance with insistence. They impress the buyer with knowledge of the product rather than with understanding of the need. Total communication and patience to wait for the perfect time make a successful salesperson.

PSP: *How do you motivate other people?*

Proctor: I'm not sure I do as good a job of this as I could. Sometimes, I tend to assume that proximity alone is enough. I get frustrated that my people cannot pick up what I'm feeling by osmosis. I feel I can pick up on their vibes. Then I realize that it is a function of the limitation of time. I try to remember that each person in one's life deserves personal time. When I feel that is needed I give it. People cannot execute a concept they do not understand. Beyond that, sharing the music is the best way to get people to dance.

PSP: *What motivates you?*

Proctor: I have been blessed with the most gentle, supportive human being on earth for a son. I have been fortunate to have touched the lives of many people who have invested in me a lot of their energies, their dreams, their goals. Quite simply, I am needed. There is no greater motivation than that.

9

Mastering the Art of Motivation

Tom Hopkins

"You have got to have a work plan, and the best time to complete it is the night before. That way you'll wake up motivated and you won't be floundering around for half a day just defining what you want to accomplish."

Everyone in the sales field knows Tom Hopkins. The boyish dynamo of the platform seems to be everywhere these days. Maybe that's because Hopkins *is* the motivator of the 1980s. But, as I found out when I interviewed him, he's much more than just another motivational mentor. Hopkins knows selling inside out. That's one of the major reasons why his platform speeches and seminars are so popular and successful.

When I interviewed Tom, we talked about many facets of his career. He dedicates himself totally to helping other people achieve at least some of the success he has seen. Tom believes in the inner power we all have to exceed our own best performance. He doesn't ask us to set goals that are unreasonable, but he does ask us to perform just a little bit above what we are accustomed to.

I was surprised by the sheer volume of travel on Hopkins' calendar. He criss-crosses this country, as well as a few others, continually, bringing the message to the faithful, like a guru of good performance. Other trainers sometimes poke fun at his unique style, at the way he adds a question to the end of any statement just to get feedback, at his high-powered pitch from the stage. But no one comes even close to matching the enormous success that meets him at every stop of the Hopkins train.

He works hard, he studies the market's needs, he covers all the essentials, and he has style. I've watched a Tom Hopkins performance from the audience and I've been ready to jump up and holler for more. His enthusiasm is infectious and his warmth is easily felt.

Hours after I finished this interview, I still felt the cadences of his speech and the message underneath. Motivators are special people—people whom we have to get close to, people whom we have to touch in some way, people whom we rely on to help us through the hard times, people who tell us that we deserve the good times. It somehow sounds more acceptable coming from someone else, and when that someone is Tom Hopkins, it sounds downright reasonable. We *can* do it, we *must* do it, we *will* do it.

The secrets that Hopkins imparts are no secrets at all. Given the appropriate professional skills, the tools to perform with, and the right motivation to set us off, we can, will, and must succeed. Just as he has.

"I learned a long time ago," says the ultra-successful sales trainer, best-selling author, and motivator, "that selling is the highest paid hard work—and the lowest paid easy work I could find. I also learned that the choice was all mine." Hopkins decided on the hard-work path and his efforts have paid off handsomely for himself and for the thousands upon thousands he has helped. On average he trains about 100,000 salespeople a year, both in the Unites States and abroad, while he earns a cool $10,000 every time he sets foot on stage to do his thing.

What he does is worth it. Covering every conceivable aspect of selling, from "applied presentation skills" to "closing zeal," Hopkins' mottos, "Money is good" and "Champions love people and use money, not the other way around," are like initiation rites, rally-style. "My goal," explains Hopkins, "is to change the image that most people have of the salesperson who just wants to cram a product down the prospect's throat. The average American today is more sophisticated and wants to buy from someone with understanding and warmth." "No one wants to be sold," he goes on philosophically, "but they do want to own things."

In Hopkins' view, salespeople can relate to him because, of all the downs they may have had, he has had at least as many, maybe more. "Self-motivation is one of the salesperson's most important tools," he claims, explaining that "there is no substitute for product knowledge and sales technique, but without a positive self-image all is lost." Hopkins believes that salespeople in particular must learn to benefit from adversity and failure. He sums up what he has learned about success by saying, in characteristically positive tones, "I am not judged by the number of times I fail, but by the number of times I succeed. And that is in direct proportion to the number of times I can fail and keep on trying."

PSP: *How do you define motivation?*
Hopkins: To me, motivation is the ability to get people to

stretch further than they are accustomed to in order to reach their goals.

PSP: *Is motivation the same for everyone?*

Hopkins: No. Motivation is different for different types of people. Some people are self-motivated. They have the ability to reach within themselves for the strengths to do what they really don't want to do, but may have to do in order to reach their desired goals.

PSP: *What are some of the other types of people?*

Hopkins: There are others who need someone to sit down with them on a periodic basis and review their goals and achievements and give them praise and recognition to further motivate them. Then you also have a certain number of people who don't want to change. Motivation for them becomes a negative force.

PSP: *How do you mean that?*

Hopkins: You cannot change people who do not want to change. You can only effect a change in someone who is ready for it. If you try to change people who are not ready, they will resist, producing a force counterproductive to motivation. They will use all their energies in a negative way.

PSP: *Would you agree that people who do not want to change will get short-changed?*

Hopkins: Yes, I would. I also find that people have to be at a certain point in their lives. The ones who have done their best in a self-motivated environment have something to prove to somebody, even if that person is the individual himself.

PSP: *In your view, what do they have to prove?*

Hopkins: They have a tremendous desire to either prove themselves to others or to themselves, or to accomplish something they haven't done before. They have an innate need to grow beyond their present parameters.

PSP: *Who motivated you at the beginning of your career?*

Hopkins: I think I fall right into that category we just talked about—I had something to prove.

PSP: *To yourself?*

Hopkins: Both to myself and to my father. He wanted me to be a famous attorney and I only lasted for 90 days in college. When I quit, I came home to tell my father and he was very disappointed and said, "I will always love you even though you'll never amount to anything."

PSP: *How did you feel about that?*

Hopkins: To me this was a tremendous emotional and psychological motivator because I told myself, "O.K., I'm going to prove I can become a success."

PSP: *How did you accomplish that goal?*

Hopkins: I went into construction and although I was making a pretty decent wage at the age of 17, I still wasn't satisfied. At 18, I decided to try sales. Even there I had a problem. I had to take the real estate exam twice.

PSP: *What was your motivation at that time?*

Hopkins: I wanted to win. If there was any kind of a contest, say for a trophy, that meant more to me than the money. If there was a vacation contest, I went after that. And then, all of a sudden, my life became a series of little victories, because I began to win—to reach my goals.

PSP: *Was there a big growth step that happened at some point?*

Hopkins: In 1968 I set a goal to sell more homes than anyone else had ever sold in one year. When I reached that goal, I started thinking about management.

PSP: *How do you sum up the effects of this desire to prove something?*

Hopkins: If a person doesn't have something to prove—or doesn't have a tremendous need or desire—it's easy to just coast along.

PSP: *Your example with your father is a good one. Did he use that same technique to motivate you when you were younger?*

Hopkins: He started out like a lot of parents. He always would say that if I didn't get a degree I wouldn't amount to anything. He was kind of a perfectionist.

PSP: *So he would exert a slight pressure by informing you of the consequences of a certain action or lack of it?*

Hopkins: Sure. The greatest motivator is either the fear of losing something or the fear of having something bad happen to you. A lot of good managers use fear properly to motivate people.

PSP: *Who or what motivates you now?*

Hopkins: Well, now I feel almost an obligation to help other people realize their goals. We're all motivated by different things—money, achievement, recognition, security, acceptance of others, love of family, self-acceptance or becoming our own person, and feeling satisfied with life.

PSP: *What demotivates people?*

Hopkins: People who are demotivated are suffering from things like self-doubt. They may fear that they won't be able to achieve their goals, or they may be listening to negative voices from outside themselves. This can affect a person's mind and attitude.

PSP: *So fear of failure can be a demotivator?*

Hopkins: Yes. Some people are so afraid of failing that they won't even try. They've been defeated before they attempt anything—defeated by their own lack of confidence or loss of sense of security. They won't take any risk at all and the last step of demotivation is the immobilization that comes from their inability to change.

PSP: *For many people there has been a significant experience with or because of some hero that has been a motivating factor. Did you have a hero who motivated you?*

Hopkins: Yes, I did. His name was J. Douglas Edwards. I consider him to have been the father of American selling. When I was 19 I spent the last $150 I had to go to a five-day training that he was conducting.

PSP: *Why did you decide to do that?*

Hopkins: Well, you see, I had failed miserably when I started in selling. It goes back to the fact that I hadn't had any training. Now, J. Douglas Edwards' intensive five-day training literally taught me what I call the art of closing the sale.

PSP: *And what did you learn?*

Hopkins: I learned all the steps to go through to qualify a prospect and sell the product.

PSP: *Did Edwards' course make a great difference in your professional life?*

Hopkins: Yes, it did, and he became my hero. I found that I wanted to become a top producer and I also wanted to earn his esteem. He became one of the main forces in my life.

PSP: *And later in your life were there other motivating forces?*

Hopkins: After Edwards I really didn't have another hero for a long time. But, I read an enormous amount—authors like Dr. Norman Vincent Peale and Zig Ziglar. These people have really done such a tremendous job for the world. I studied the art of selling, and, after I sold the real estate office I had managed, I decided that I wanted to teach. It's been very motivating working to help others realize their goals the way Edwards helped me realize mine.

PSP: *What suggestions do you have for sales managers or trainers who want to motivate others to realize their goals?*

Hopkins: I think the first important step is to help other people set their own goals. These goals have to be better than what the person is currently doing, but they still have to be believable.

PSP: *How does the manager do that?*

Hopkins: Well, every manager should sit down with a new salesperson and ask him or her questions right in the beginning; not just talk, but actually ask specific questions, such as, "I'd like you to answer some questions—would you like me to help you reach your goal?" And then, "Let's outline a couple of goals that would make you happy—what kind of a car would you really like to have in the next year or two?" And the manager should write that down in the salesperson's folder. They should do it together, and then outline other goals, like the kind of house the salesperson might want to be living in over the next two or three years and so on.

PSP: *How many goals should the manager help the salesperson set?*

Hopkins: I think about five or six. Other goals would include what income for the first year's work would make the salesperson feel he or she had done a really good job. Get the salesperson to commit himself or herself to specific and measurable goals and to make the two, the manager and the salesperson, partners in that effort.

PSP: *What would you do then?*

Hopkins: Then I would ask, "Do you want me to help you reach those goals?" I would get a commitment.

PSP: *Is there a step after the commitment?*

Hopkins: Yes, you must get that person's permission, an indication that he or she is ready to have you help him or her reach those goals in very specific ways, by showing what the person is doing right and wrong and by helping improve professional performance. That's the tough part. You say, "If need be, would you allow me to sit down with you and make suggestions, critique and advise you on what you need to do to reach the goals we've just outlined?"

PSP: *You get permission to act as a mentor?*

Hopkins: Yes. And also as a disciplinarian if necessary. I then go a step further. I think the manager has to write down two agreements. One is, "I hereby agree to do whatever is necessary to help John Smith reach the outlined goals." Then I sign my name. Then I ask John Smith to write down that he agrees to let me do whatever is necessary to help him reach those goals.

PSP: *So you make a counter-commitment to the goals that you've set together?*

Hopkins: That's right. Now, if John Smith is sitting around down in the dumps three months later, the manager can say, "Look, you're not making enough calls and contacting enough people. You've got to do more prospecting." Now both the salesperson and the manager are interdependent and have made a commitment in writing to work together so it's unlikely that the salesperson is either going to resent the manager's advice, or feel threatened by it. He is more likely to act on it and to succeed in his profession.

PSP: *So a good manager acts as a guide, a disciplinarian, a mentor, and a teacher?*

Hopkins: That's the way I see the manager's role. But, also, a manager should do some research into the past of the new salesperson. He or she should know what that salesperson was making before and what they already have in terms of lifestyle. Most people don't make drastic lifestyle changes. If someone is driving a $10,000 car and says she wants to be driving a $40,000 car in a year, the manager's role is to help her define a more realistic goal that is reachable and reasonable, and maybe put the higher goal down the road a few years. Most people grow gradually, and that's healthy.

PSP: *How about the superstar who comes in and really outperforms all the manager's expectations?*

Hopkins: That happens, but it's only about one in a thousand. For the rest of the salespeople out there, goals that are unrealistic can lead to a despondent attitude, and that's very demotivating.

PSP: *Big fantasies can end up in big disappointments?*

Hopkins: Yes. You've got to have a work plan, and the best time to complete it is the night before. That way you'll wake up motivated and you won't be floundering around for half a day just defining what you want to accomplish.

PSP: *What would be another technique?*

Hopkins: Don't get in a rut. I tell people to vary their routines—maybe to not wake up at the same time every day, to not drive the same way to work or to their territory. In other words, don't confine yourself. New things to look at and new ways of doing things lead to new ideas, and new ideas lead to an expanded horizon. Expanding your horizons automatically leads to bigger success.

PSP: *What do you do to stay motivated in your own life?*

Hopkins: I strongly believe that you have to live what you teach. I do all the things we've talked about here. Plus, I believe, as they say in show business, the show must go on. If I've flown from one time zone to another, and I'm tired, I still go ahead as planned, and I find that once you get up there in front of people who are looking to you for help, you have to give the best you've got. When you're giving your best, like a salesperson talking with a customer, and you're not feeling that good, you start faking it and, suddenly, you're actually making it. Your adrenalin kicks in and you really do feel good, and you're doing a good job.

PSP: *What do you think about the negative aspects of selling—like rejection?*

Hopkins: You can't take rejection personally. That's the cardinal rule. The only way you can manage your feelings about rejection is to change your attitude toward the word no. If you have to talk to five people to get one order, and you earn $100 every time you get an order, then each no is worth $25 because out of five you'll get four no's and one yes. Instead of getting depressed each time you hear no, you say, "Thanks for the $25," and make the next call.

PSP: *Do you teach any other mental attitude boosters?*

Hopkins: I ask students of my courses to memorize things like: "I never see failure as failure, but only as a learning experience," or, "I never see failure as failure, but only as the negative feedback I need to change course in my direction."

PSP: *What do you call these?*

Hopkins: I call them the "Attitudes Toward Failure."

PSP: *Are there more?*

Hopkins: Yes. "I never see failure as failure, but only as an opportunity to develop my sense of humor," or, "only as part of a game I must play to win." The last is, "Selling and business and life are all a big percentage game."

PSP: *What was your most demotivating experience?*

Hopkins: When I was just starting out I sold four homes, all contingent on one of them going to a close. I worked for three months on that transaction. They all fell through and I made nothing—absolutely zero.

PSP: *Then what happened?*

Hopkins: After my second year, my income started to increase and things began to improve. I changed strategy, I started to train others, and the challenges got bigger and I was able to meet them with success.

PSP: *What was your most motivating experience?*

Hopkins: Oh, when my book, *How to Master the Art of Selling*, hit the best-seller list, without a doubt.

PSP: *Why was that such a great thing for you?*

Hopkins: Well, when I dropped out of college after 90 days, and then wrote a book that people thought worthy enough to buy so many copies that it hit the best-seller list, that was really motivating. Then I was invited to speak in front of 150 college professors on how to motivate students—a college dropout on motivating students. I did a three-hour session on how to help the students out of a study slump. I wrote the whole session for the professors. To have them sit there and take notes and then give me a standing ovation when I was done was the highlight of this college dropout's life so far.

PSP: *So for you motivation comes from helping other people to grow?*

Hopkins: I had 10 or 15 letters from people who went out and increased their incomes after going through one of my courses, but I had one letter in particular. A woman wrote that she had just come out of the hospital after suffering a stroke. Half her body is paralyzed, but she went out after the course and in the first year made almost $50,000. Stories like that motivate me to spend 95 percent of my time travelling from seminar to seminar teaching my students how to become champions.

PSP: *What is your measure of success?*

Hopkins: My measure of success is to reach fulfillment in four areas. Number one is financial accomplishments, based on my own self-image and goals. Number two is emotional stability and the ability to control emotional handicaps in my own life. Number three is physical fitness and feeling good physically. And number four is maintaining my spiritual awareness and my personal relationship with a higher power. If you can do all four of these, you're a successful human being by my measure of success.

PSP: *There's always a tendency to go out of those bounds every day.*

Hopkins: Certainly, and it's a constant struggle, isn't it?

10

The Successful Motivation Machine

C. Steven McMillan

"There is nothing less motivating than a tremendous amount of rhetoric that is not supported by genuine opportunity."

Every year the Direct Sales Association has a big meeting for all its top brass. Every company in the direct sales field is represented. When I decided to go to the 1985 meeting, it was to meet with and interview C. Steven McMillan, chairman and CEO of Electrolux Corporation. At the last moment McMillan cancelled because of other commitments and there I was, four hours of driving behind me, no interview in sight, and the hotel swarming with direct-selling executives.

I called McMillan's room, spoke to his wife, and asked if she might convey to him how much our readers would appreciate McMillan sharing his knowledge and experience. I also mentioned in passing that I had driven four hours just to see him. A few moments later the interview was rescheduled and we met shortly thereafter. Our meeting was marked by the enthusiasm of the convention and I was excited to hear McMillan's sound approach to selling and motivation—an approach that has worked extremely well for the company and for him.

Although he didn't have tigers or hot air balloons with him, I found it easy to imagine this Harvard-trained executive onstage with his head between a tiger's jaws. It's the sort of picture one associates with a carnival rather than a board room, and one can almost hear the clucking tongues of McMillan's Harvard Business School professors lamenting about all that upper-echelon management training being used in a floor show. But this man, who claims that the only way to solve difficulties is to have a plan, also knows how to rally his troops—make them stand up and cheer. He has orchestrated lavish productions to launch sales contests or to reward winners who achieved or went beyond their goals. He sees a place for everyone in direct selling—an opportunity to do something. Salespeople can set their own goals, reach them at their own pace, and gain satisfaction—just by getting out there in the field.

McMillan is a manager who leads by example. He faces problems squarely. And he encourages his subordinates to do the same. He is well aware of the magic quality of hype, but he knows that hype alone will never sell a thing. Without training and skills, no product will ever be moved. The bonus trips, the conventions in exotic locales that Electrolux features for its top producers, and the extravaganzas it produces are all part of the hype machine. McMillan does it well. But he also watches the management side. His professors should be proud. Steve McMillan is a rare blend of showman and manager. I don't remember ever having met someone in whom the two qualities were so complementary.

"When I'm faced with a problem," says Steven McMillan, chairman and CEO of Electrolux Corporation," "the odds are that I'm going to solve it." These are positive words, and McMillan has good reason to be optimistic. In each of the first three years after taking over the number-one spot at Electrolux, the company achieved record sales. On top of this, 1,000 branch managers in the United States and Canada have racked up an impressive 25 percent rise in income. On the profit side, the picture is even rosier for McMillan's door-to-door army. "But," warns the management specialist, "I am as capable as any other CEO of making any set of numbers look good in the short run. The real test of the success of my management team is what happens three years from now."

"I may be right, and then again I may at times be entirely wrong in my solutions to problems," McMillan says with a candor that characterizes his total professionalism, "but I take tremendous comfort in knowing that I am capable of dealing with issues." This then is Steve McMillan's motivational forte. He knows he doesn't have to worry about problems, that he can face them head on because he has a methodology for dealing with them. "The most frightening thing in the world is not knowing what to do next," he says.

His position as the top decision-maker seems to have benefitted both the CEO of Electrolux and the sales team he supports. When asked how he motivates others around him, McMillan is quick to point out the weaknesses of pep rallies alone: "We do a lot of what I call the "hype" meetings, like the big rally we did recently in Bermuda. I was the first CEO of this company to enhance the image of the Electrolux mascot, the tiger, by coming out on stage with a live 500-pound Siberian named Bombay. I stuck my head in his mouth and everything. So I agree that there's a place for hype. But without a methodology for solving problems and facing issues, the hype alone will backfire."

In this exclusive interview with PSP, Chairman and CEO McMillan discusses his motivation techniques and his methodology for success.

PSP: *Who motivated you when you were young?*
McMillan: My parents were very supportive, yet had high ambitions for me. But I always felt that most of the motivation I had came from within. I actually feel that if you want to motivate yourself the best way is to go out and try to motivate someone else.

PSP: *Did you have any experiences as a boy growing up that helped to motivate you?*
McMillan: I remember feeling very concerned about making transitions when I was young. Moving from junior high to high school, moving to a new town, I wondered, would I be as popular as before, would I have any friends, would I be as good a ball player? I was nervous that the competition would be much harder and then I wondered, would I fail? Fear of failure was a great motivator for me.

PSP: *How did you overcome that?*
McMillan: Well, when I went from a high school that graduated 120 people to a university with 15,000 students I focussed on my own need for self-expression—which was really a need to have an impact on things. The great fear was that I was now out of my league. This was even stronger when I went to the Navy Supply Corps school, where I had classmates from Yale, Harvard, and Princeton. They read *The New York Times* from front to back every day. It was the biggest newspaper I had ever seen. I was very intimidated by these students, but I was still motivated to find my position.

PSP: *What has been the most motivating experience so far in your life?*
McMillan: I remember one in particular when I was up in Edmonton, Canada. I'd been up there as president of Electro-

lux Canada for only six months or so and was not acclimated to the extreme cold in the winter. One morning we were going to drive out to a branch where I had to give a little morning talk that was supposed to be inspirational and motivational. We had to get up at 5:00 in the morning to get there in time, and I remember having a sense of depression about having to get up that early in the pitch-dark and drive an hour and a half in the bitter cold. I got up and showered, and when I came out of my room I must have had the look of a totally defeated and disgusted soul. My head was down. I was dragging my suitcases.

Just as I walked through my door, a guy coming out of the room across the hall said, "Good morning, how are you?" in this tremendously upbeat, enthusiastic voice. My reaction was that of a typical Scrooge, and I looked up at him and suddenly remembered the wake-up call that I had gotten, and the cheerful female voice that had said, "Good morning, Mr. McMillan, it's 5:30 and the temperature is 14 degrees below zero—have a nice day." I had said to myself, "You've got to be kidding. How can you have a nice day if it's 14 below? I could die just walking to the car." But this guy was so upbeat that I took a shot and said, "You're up awfully early, aren't you?" And he answered, "Yeah, I love to get out there before the sun's up." "Do you realize," I asked him, "that it's 14 degrees below zero and you could die of windchill in probably a minute of two out there this morning?"

Do you know what he said to me? He said, "Yeah, I'm going to have to move quick today." We then walked down the corridor together and got into the elevator on the 18th floor, and then stopped on the 16th, and this guy got in who looked just the way I must have looked when I came out of my room. And we both greeted him enthusiastically, as we did another on the 12th floor and one more on the 8th. When we got off at the lobby the bellhop said to us, "Boy, you guys must have had some party last night!" The enthusiasm of one man had rubbed off on all of us and we were all ready to "move quick out there." I think the moral is that you *can* affect other people, and very frequently it involves no more than the positiveness of your own attitude.

PSP: *What is positive thinking to you?*

McMillan: To me it is to always look for the good things. If there is a single message that I try to communicate and to live by it is that you've got to find the positives. It is totally a waste of your time to dwell on the negatives, even though they will always be there.

PSP: *What do you do with the negatives?*

McMillan: There are problems that we deal with all the time. We don't ignore them. We have to face those problems head on. But there is a difference between letting the problem overwhelm you and operating under the assumption that you will win.

PSP: *So you are saying that positive thinking is more than just putting a positive face on any situation.*

McMillan: That's right. For instance, I don't think I would be effective as a motivational speaker because I wouldn't be able to track the results. As a CEO I've got to think about my business and my people and how they are going to do two, three, five, and even ten years from now—not just whether they are fired up immediately after a talk. They need enthusiasm, clearly, but my job is to give them much more.

PSP: *At the present time, how many salespeople does Electrolux have?*

McMillan: Right now we have about 28,000.

PSP: *How do you see your obligation for motivating those 28,000 salespeople?*

McMillan: Our most important obligation to motivate our salespeople is to make sure there is sufficient opportunity for them. There is nothing less motivating than a tremendous amount of rhetoric that is not supported by a genuine opportunity.

PSP: *So the opportunity comes first?*

McMillan: Yes. The fundamental structures have to be there first. History is full of companies that over-invested in inspirational rhetoric. There has to be an economic basis so that if the salesperson is genuinely motivated and applies him- or herself, and follows the steps, the rewards will be there in the end.

PSP: *And once the realistic opportunity is there, what are the next steps?*

McMillan: To achieve genuine motivation, you've got to marry several things together. First there's the opportunity, as we've discussed. Second, a clear business objective has to be there. Third, the how-to skills have to be there. And, finally, there's the hype.

PSP: *By hype do you mean sales contests and the like?*

McMillan: Yes. Our meeting in Bermuda, which was organized by Radio City Music Hall Productions, is a perfect example of hype. I think it's fun and exciting, but alone it will not get the job done.

PSP: *Is this practice of adding selling skills to the hype an Electrolux concept?*

McMillan: Here at Electrolux we often say that motivation without education equals frustration.

PSP: *Where do goals fit with your motivation picture?*

McMillan: In the business objective—that's where you put the goal setting. You have to make sure that the business objective is not too difficult, but it also has to be defined in such a way that it stretches the individual. Our salespeople, as well as managers, have a role in defining that. But if they don't stretch themselves, they'll never learn the process of managing themselves.

PSP: *How do you know when you have been successful in motivating someone?*

McMillan: What I want for my salespeople is for them to find the level at which they are comfortable and then move above it. But they need to define the satisfaction they want—we are all different in what we define as success. If the tools are provided and we can stimulate meaningful action, then we have been successful. My objective is to insure that all elements of motivation are present.

PSP: *Who are you more interested in, the heroes of sales, or*

the ordinary salespeople who are having a hard time of it?
McMillan: I'm concerned about the majority of people. The superstars will always rise to the top. But we, as a company, should focus on making it more likely that the majority will raise their performances to higher levels. I want to give them something that they can use. I want to tell them some specific things that they can do to sell in this business. They all need a game plan.
PSP: *What is the most demotivating thing that salespeople can do?*
McMillan: Worry. It is the single most unrewarding of all human emotions. It does not accomplish a thing. There is absolutely no positive result from worrying, yet all of us do it from time to time.
PSP: *Why do you think salespeople worry?*
McMillan: They worry because they come up against a problem and they have no methodology for dealing with it. Worrying won't solve a problem. But if you say, "I have identified a problem, or an issue, or here's an obstacle we have to get over," I'll say, "Fine, let's look at that from an analytical point of view. Let's think about what our options are." Thinking through the process is what's important. It is very rewarding if people have a methodology for dealing with problems. This usually involves nothing more than thinking through them rather than panicking.
PSP: *From your experience, do most salespeople face problems squarely?*
McMillan: Most explode problems way beyond what they really represent. The reason these problems really become overwhelming is because there is no methodology to define what the problem is. You cannot solve any problem without analyzing it. But worrying about it just wastes your time and energy.
PSP: *And once a salesperson has learned to approach problems from this analytical point, what happens then?*
McMillan: Once they have learned an approach they can then

solve their own problems, and that is very rewarding for them and for me as a motivator. There is nothing more frightening than fear of the unknown.

PSP: *What are other demotivators that you see?*

McMillan: Obviously the pressures of life can weigh on people. Or they can be physically tired. You have to learn how to pace yourself. And then to develop a certain comfort level in dealing with recurring situations.

PSP: *When you are motivating salespeople, do you have a total picture in your mind of what you're after?*

McMillan: I want the company to grow and I also want our people to grow and prosper individually. I care about them as individuals, but it would be wrong to call me a humanist, because I know that if they don't prosper we as a company do not grow. The two are inextricably linked.

PSP: *What have you learned in your years of running a direct sales company that would be helpful to other sales managers?*

McMillan: The importance of a broad definition of what motivation is can't be minimized. I was very much on the hype side before. When I first started out I thought that you just go in there and wave that flag and rally the troops. We still have hype, like the 500-pound Electrolux tiger I carry around to meetings and rallies. I stick my head in that tiger's mouth, we fly off in hot air balloons, but I know that by itself the showmanship won't help sales.

PSP: *What will?*

McMillan: Market research, improved selling skills, better problem solving methodology, management training. These are all integral parts of motivation.

PSP: *Do you think that sales is a career with a high degree of self-worth attached to it?*

McMillan: If I were to do a survey of all the high schools in any state, I'm sure that not a lot of young people would list selling vacuum cleaners door-to-door in their top ten priorities for the future. And not everybody is willing to pay the price to make a very high income. But in selling, it's really up to the individual and that's the major benefit. If I can help my salespeople to see that, then I've motivated them.

PSP: *What is your measure of success?*

McMillan: I guess more than anything else I am addicted to influence. It is very important to me to be in a position where I can have a major impact in terms of people. The motivation to expand that influence is rather constant.

A Letter to the Boss

"Recently I got a letter from one of our salespeople who had just retired after working for 32 years for Electrolux," says company chairman McMillan. "This man took the elements of what we have to offer and he molded them to what he wanted to accomplish in his own life." Although McMillan is sure that the man's name would never have appeared on the company roster of the top ten salespeople, he is proud that his company offered an opportunity for him and any others who want it to make a contribution and to live a full life. "To me," says McMillan, "that's the essence of what we want to do in motivation."

Dear Mr. McMillan,

Since I retired last year I've meant to write you to express my gratitude to the company. For nearly 32 years, almost half my lifetime, I was a member of the sales force and held no other job. For 18 of those years I was an assistant sales manager and field manager. I was a branch manager for one year.

I derived great satisfaction in helping others to success. Though never in the high-income brackets, my earnings were sufficient to enable me to make outside investments and retire in comfort. Electrolux offers three kinds of opportunity. One is higher-than-average income, another is the opportunity for rapid advancement, and the last is the opportunity for personal freedom. I opted for personal freedom. I believe that I was most successful; I was able to live a life I wanted. What greater success could there be?

My goal in life is to travel. The joy of travel is the main binding force of my marriage. In the past years my wife and I have visited all 50 states, every province and territory of Canada, plus Guatemala, the Bahamas, and half the states of Mexico. We have sailed around Africa, and around the world, travelled across Europe, through France, Turkey, and Greece. We explored Australia's outback, and have journeyed to China and Tibet.

Thanks to Electrolux, it has been a good life and my wife and I wish to express our sincere appreciation.

The Electrolux Motivation Machine

When the Electrolux Corporation motivates the top performers from its sales force of 28,000, it's no holds barred—everyone walks away excited. At two typical rallies, one at the splendid Hyatt Regency Waikiki, the other staged at Bermuda's plush Princess Hotel, dancers, singers, and musical extravaganzas topped the bill. But don't get the idea that it's just "sit back and be motivated." With awards, banquets, fireworks, and songs from the hometowns of some of the top producers, everyone got into the act.

Barnett Lipman, producer of Electrolux motivational super-rallies, explains, "Our services for the convention run the gamut from theme and script development, stage direction, original lyric composition, and choreography—all put together for a custom stage event relating to the Electrolux theme of 'cleaning up a dirty town and cleaning out the competition.'" Radio City Music Hall Productions, long known for its electric and professional productions, went all out to feature state-of-the-art audiovisual and video support systems.

The Electrolux Hawaiian and Bermuda rallies marked a new high in motivational rallies for the purpose of rewarding a hard-working sales force that delivers the bottom line. From the planes chartered just to bring the show and its equipment to the rally site, to top talent performances by Loretta Lynn and Glenn Campbell, the shows never missed a beat. The awesome figures involved make an inaugural day in Washington look like a kiddie show. The cost (more than $1 million), the people (65 for production and stage crew), and then the salespeople, who are the honored guests, have to be worked into the entire production.

In the end, what holds the whole show together is the music. Music makes the people cry and gets them on their feet applauding. Music from their hometowns makes them proud, and music makes them feel at one with each other. Husbands and wives, who've travelled to the rallies at the company's expense, stand next to each other, sing, cry, laugh, and applaud their own and everyone else's efforts. It makes for great memories, and great motivation too. And, in case you're wondering how you top all of this for a dynamite finish, try *two* tigers flanking the chairman of the board at center stage, followed by a tremendous fireworks display.

11

Solution-Oriented Selling

F. G. "Buck" Rodgers

"IBM doesn't sell products. At IBM, people sell solutions to a set of problems."

If there's one company that exemplifies successful selling in this century, it is IBM Corporation. One of the significant contributors to that success, as VP of marketing, was F. G. "Buck" Rodgers. When I spoke with Buck about his lifelong experience with IBM, I was impressed by his professionalism, his candor, and his creative approach to the same problems that everyone in selling faces. Rodgers' ability to move an audience was an invaluable asset during his tenure with IBM, but his dogged determination to solve the customer's problem was probably what won him his executive title and his many successes.

An old selling adage says, "You can get anything you want in life providing you help enough other people get what they want." The author of that motto is Zig Ziglar, but IBM, with Rodgers at the marketing helm, developed the concept into a corporate way of life.

During the interview, Rodgers' voice carried an air of intensity whenever we touched on the responsibility of the company to help the customer solve problems, whether they involved budgets, inventory, or delivery. The more complex and competitive our society has become, the more important it is for customers to feel their needs are recognized, their problems addressed, and workable solutions presented. Buck Rodgers exemplifies this solution-oriented approach to selling.

Rodgers is a team player, the more so now that he is on his own. He still promotes the concepts that have been so successful at IBM. He speaks to university and business audiences all over the country about what goes into the making of an effective and efficient model of marketing and management. In my experience, an all-around manager like Buck Rodgers is hard to find. It is to IBM's further credit that its management team is constantly investing millions of dollars in training and retraining executives at every level of the organization. IBM employees have to think of themselves as perpetual students, partly because the markets they service are constantly changing.

I thought I knew what it meant to be a professional salesperson. After our interview with Buck Rodgers, I found myself studying the basics all over again. I realized that the only way to advance is by continually improving our mastery of the basics.

Thirty-five years ago, F. G. (Buck) Rodgers began what turned out to be an illustrious career with the then-smallish (sales of $250 million) IBM Corporation. The year was 1950, the country was on the verge of rockin' 'round the clock with Bill Haley and the Comets, and the personal computer had not yet been invented. It was a world waiting for the explosion of the electronic microchip age, and Buck Rodgers was to be one of the knights of its untarnished top brass.

"It was an exciting time," says Rodgers, "and I was one of the few marketing experts in 'stored program machines' " (computers). Rodgers sold the smaller version of this engineering marvel for two years before getting his first big break. He captained the team that installed one of the first large-scale computers, an IBM 705, in a Westinghouse Electric plant in Sharon, Pennsylvania. It took up thousands of square feet and relied on vacuum-tube technology. "Today," chuckles IBM's former vice-president of marketing, "my little PC is more powerful than that behemoth was."

The year and a half it took for installation and the 90-day shake-down after it was in, plus the success of the whole operation, caught the eye of IBM's executive vice-president, L. H. Lamotte. Rodgers' soon became administrative assistant to one of IBM's builders, and the rest, as they say, is history.

"From him, I learned to clearly articulate what it was I wanted people to accomplish," Rodgers says. Following in his mentor's path, Rodgers never set more than five goals at any one time, and never delegated more than that magic number to any subordinate either. "You have to make the choice," explains Rodgers, "between desirability and necessity."

It was during an early stint as branch sales manager that Rodgers developed the belief that a company's organizational structure should be inverted, with the customer at the top and sales reps and management underneath. Rodgers' commitment to the customer even went so far as to give priority to appointments with customers when they conflicted with meetings in the IBM executive suite.

Rodgers once promised an aircraft manufacturer in Seattle that, if it would buy the IBM product, he would personally fly there every 30 days for six straight months to insure the success of a complex computer installation. That condition helped make the sale, and Rodgers kept his word. He is a man given to keeping his word, showing up for meetings on time, and remembering appointments. Since his retirement from IBM, Buck Rodgers has written a book entitled The IBM Way *(New York: Harper & Row, 1986).*

In this exclusive interview, Buck Rodgers talks about the IBM that he has known for thirty-five years; about the past and the present, about what makes it one of the greatest institutions of our age, and the part that he has played in this long running corporate hit.

PSP: *Since the year you began your career, tens of thousands of marketing people were hired by IBM in the United States. What do you think allowed you to go to the very top marketing position in the company?*

Rodgers: There were two things—commitment and integrity. I never failed to meet objectives, I never failed to be on time for meetings. I tried to do the little things well and the customers always knew they could count on me. So could the people I worked with at IBM. They didn't have to write me a lot of letters to get things done. The same is still true today. People who call me on the phone with a problem know it's going to be taken care of.

PSP: *When you were hired, was it your dream to one day be the top marketing person at IBM?*

Rodgers: No, that came after I had been through several field assignments. I hoped someday to be president of IBM's computer operations. But I decided that the only way to achieve that was to do the best job in each position I held.

PSP: *That's a good attitude to have.*

Rodgers: I have always had a positive attitude. I feel there isn't any problem that can't be solved with common sense and a little sweat.

PSP: *How do you develop this winning attitude?*

Rodgers: A lot of it comes from inside the individual. But there are ways you can bring out a person's innate strengths. For myself, I have always had a talent for speaking. I never use any notes or a podium. I walk around. I've never had any special training. But public speaking is an ability that I have developed and made good use of.

PSP: *So, developing a special talent in one area will help you in other areas?*

Rodgers: Yes, always, but you need the desire to excel—at least to live up to one's own expectations. A lot of my success has been luck and a lot of it turns out to be that I performed in an exemplary way in every job I was given. I wasn't afraid to fail.

PSP: *Did your parents instill a strong desire in you to be an achiever or a winner? To be somebody?*

Rodgers: Yes, I think they did. All my life I played sports. I was all-state in football, captain of the basketball team, president of the class for four years. I played football in college and today I run five miles, six times a week, and I'm an avid golfer and tennis player. I sort of compete with myself, but not to an obsessive point.

PSP: *It sounds like you derive a pleasure and satisfaction from being fully functioning!*

Rodgers: I agree with that. I spend a lot of time on college campuses talking about changing values. I think people are trying to find the right balance in their lives. They expect to work for fair wages, but they don't want to sacrifice family life for their jobs. I also feel it's important to pay what I call "civic rent." To me, this is teaching young people. To others it may be involvement in programs dealing with drug abuse or mental health. Balance is important in life and I think people at all ages are seeking that today.

PSP: *The IBM philosophy of business has become almost legendary. What makes it so special?*

Rodgers: It is based on three beliefs; first, respect for the individual; second, to give the best service of any company in the world; and third, to expect excellence from what people do. This was the idea of Tom Watson, Sr., when he started the business back in 1914. He said that if you're going to do business with the IBM Corporation, you ought to feel that you're getting value and exceptional service. It is a desire to do things right the first time that permeates the business.

PSP: *What impressed you personally about IBM?*

Rodgers: When I was being interviewed in college, I had never heard of IBM and I decided to go with them because I was intrigued by their philosophy and I was impressed with the quality of the IBM people that I met.

PSP: *You were impressed by the recruiters?*

Rodgers: IBM uses first-line managers to do the hiring, the managers who do the day-to-day jobs. If you are held accountable for results, then you ought to have the freedom to pick the people you want. IBM does that.

PSP: *Were there any myths about the company that you found were not true?*

Rodgers: There is one [*he chuckles*] and that's the IBM dress code. They don't have any policy that says you've got to wear a white shirt or a dark suit or a sincere tie. IBM really doesn't care what people look like, and I don't either, as long as they dress with taste. You want the customer to concentrate on what you're saying, not on what you look like. Even so, up until the time I retired, I wore a lot more white shirts than I did blue!

PSP: *You said that your first position at IBM was as a marketing representative. You didn't say sales rep.*

Rodgers: At IBM we called our people marketing reps. There is a distinction between marketing and selling. Selling, to me, is the art of persuasion. That's the ability through personal attributes to convince someone that they need to buy the product or service that you're offering. Marketing to me is a more all encompassing term. It means understanding the customers, speaking their language, putting together a cost-justified solution, and most of all being able to give value. IBM doesn't sell products. At IBM, people sell solutions to a set of problems. What the customer wants to know is how you can improve the inventory turnover rate, or lower costs—how you can help a business better serve its own customers.

PSP: *There are so many selling concepts in this country: non-manipulative selling, the soft sell, consultative selling, situational selling, and so on. But you seem to be zeroing in on solution-oriented selling.*

Rodgers: That's what IBM's training program is all about. You've got to speak the language that the customer understands. The days of Willy Loman are long gone—you have to go in and think, "How can I, in some way, with my thinking and my products, give value and service to this particular customer?" Those who do that are the individuals who are going to succeed.

PSP: *What are your own personal principles of persuasion— ones that work well for you?*

Rodgers: I try to be a reasonably good listener. I try to get the customer to have confidence in me as an individual. I try to convince people that I am interested in them and their problems. I share ideas and then try to get them to share theirs. Then I try to find answers to their problems. Too many times people don't get the chance to say what's on their minds. When the salesperson gives the customer the "fire hose approach," that's missing what might have been the real hot button you were looking for.

PSP: *Good listening establishes trust and confidence.*

Rodgers: But it's the hardest thing in the world to do, especially for people who have a lot of ideas and are enthusiastic. It's very difficult for all of us.

PSP: *I understand that the training program for an IBM marketing rep takes one whole year. How is it structured?*

Rodgers: The first 30-day period is an orientation into IBM's culture and history. After that, the new reps go off to Atlanta or Dallas for 30 days, where they start to learn about the products and selling techniques. Then they go back to the branch office, where they apply what they have learned in the classroom. They work with the marketing reps and systems engineers on real-life proposals, and they work with customers. After about three months, they go back to the classroom for another 30 days of application orientation, plus they find out what the competitive world is all about. During this time they are alternating between theory and practicality. IBM tries to get its marketing reps to understand the terms and conditions and the resources available to them. The entire process is very competitive and they're on their feet as much as possible. When they're through, they are totally confident about the products and the competition, and, above all, they are application oriented.

PSP: *What you seem to be saying is that this kind of totally focussed training translates into a professional solution-oriented attitude.*

Rodgers: That's right. You don't go from one level to the next at IBM until you have been tested and proven ready to make that step. It's a positive type of reinforcement. I've seen very fine organizations give little attention to initial training, let alone continuing education. If there's no structure or discipline—it won't work. We found out there are two things in a business that you increase out of proportion to the growth rate of the company: one is education, the other is communication. You train people well and communicate your goals to them.

PSP: *What is the relationship between the trainer in the classroom and the line manager in the branch office?*

Rodgers: The line manager has the responsibility to see that the individual completes the training and that he is self-sufficient. The people at the education centers are responsible for making sure that the student is getting the basic fundamentals.

PSP: *Who does the actual sales and marketing training at the centers?*

Rodgers: IBM takes the best people from their sales force, people who have an ability to express themselves, and gives them training assignments from 18 to 24 months. They become role models who can convey actual field experience. Marketing training is very sought after at IBM because it's a stepping stone to a line-management position or to moving up in the business.

PSP: *That's a very unusual concept.*

Rodgers: Most companies are reluctant to take their top producers out of the field and put them in education assignments. IBM says you must do this. Whatever the short-term effect, it will pay back tenfold by having knowledgeable representatives interfacing with the customer.

PSP: *So your best marketing reps seek out the function of trainer to go higher up the ladder?*

Rodgers: That's right. They don't get stale in the process and you keep a small number of professional educators and the rest are fresh, new, and enthusiastic.

PSP: *Any manager who has been out of selling for more than two or three years tends to get out of touch with the marketplace.*

Rodgers: IBM has a management system in which the top officers—the president, the heads of engineering/manufacturing divisions, the heads of finance, personnel—are assigned specific customers. They work with these customers, but always through the marketing rep in the branch office. This keeps top management from being in an ivory tower, out of touch with reality. The other bonus is that the branch manager can use that top executive to cut through the bureaucracy. If the branch manager needs something done, he or she can go directly to that individual. It sounds so simple, but, believe me, it's done in very few organizations.

PSP: *You coined a wonderful term and I'd like to ask you about it. You once said that people in companies sometimes suffered from "psychosclerosis."*

Rodgers: Yes—that means a "hardening of the attitudes," when people begin to feel they no longer can affect what goes on in an organization, when bureaucracy takes over. That's why IBM pulls people out of their protected little corners. The secret is to move people back and forth between various functions and disciplines. This broadens the person and provides fresh insights.

PSP: *What are some of the incentives that IBM uses to inspire sales and marketing people?*

Rodgers: First, people are paid well for what they do. IBM has a salary and incentive structure that is split approximately 50/50. It is a "pay for performance" philosophy—the more you install, the more you make. Also, IBM pays its people more than other comparable companies pay.

PSP: *And then what else do they offer?*

Rodgers: The most important is a meaningful and challenging assignment; beyond that is one of the best benefits programs in any industry. However, there is something I call the "take back." Any time a piece of equipment is discontinued or cancelled, no matter how long it has been installed for, the marketing rep who is on that account is charged back with the original commission. This makes sure that when the reps take over an account, they provide outstanding service. Most of IBM's business is based on repeat orders so the customer is only going to buy as long as he is satisfied.

PSP: *That's a tough rule.*

Rodgers: Yes, it is, but it worked for as long as I was with IBM.

PSP: *What are some of the other forms of incentive?*

Rodgers: There's the 100 Percent Club. This is important because it's the way to be recognized by peers and eventually be promoted. IBM strives to have between 70 percent and 75 percent of their people make their objectives and attend the 100 Percent Club. They also have a Golden Circle. IBM takes the top 10 percent of its sales force from around the world, with their spouses, to a five-day recognition event in exciting resort locations. It serves to recognize superior performance, but also has a marketing purpose. You hear a lot of spouses saying, "You better bring me back here next year."

PSP: *I understand that you have one other form of incentive that is very popular with the salespeople.*

Rodgers: You must be talking about what I call the Lightning Strikes program. Managers at all levels are given a dollar budget to recognize people on the spot who have demonstrated extraordinary effort. It might be for a new account or for helping a customer with a special problem. The support people can get these awards too. It's a night on the town, dinner, a show. They can range from a simple thank you to several thousand dollars handed out for unusual acts of heroism.

PSP: *It sounds like IBM is run like a small company.*

Rodgers: That's right. When IBM was small, top management ran the company as if it were big; now that IBM is big, management runs it as if it were small. For example, they never let a branch office get above a certain size. Also, every effort is made to maintain a manager-to-person ratio of about one to twelve.

PSP: *What do you think salespeople should be taught about selling that they are generally not taught?*

Rodgers: Two things come to mind. First, concentrate on what the product will do, not what it is. The customer is only interested in results. Second—develop a financial capability. Due to the wide variety of terms and conditions available today, a key part of selling business is the ability to clearly portray the right method of financial acquisition.

PSP: *Can you talk a little bit about how you helped the IBM rep identify with the total marketing philosophy?*

Rodgers: Again, the key is feedback. Every 90 days, IBM asks all of its marketing reps and systems engineers to review the organization from a customer-satisfaction perspective. They are asked to tell what they think of management's capability, quality of products, and the responsiveness of the support structure. This input is then matched against a similar set of survey questions that have been responded to by customers. This gives top management a good idea of any negative trends. The main objective is to take preventive action and correct the problems, plus to focus on the strengths.

PSP: *What was the biggest disappointment you ever suffered in your career?*

Rodgers: That's a tough question. At one point I was interested in running the IBM Corporation. That didn't happen, but it never really affected my style of management or the way I performed on a daily basis. If I ever got shot out of the saddle, and that happens to everybody, the secret was to be able to get right back on the horse. A lot of people don't do that, they get gun shy instead. They start to worry and play it safe. You have to expect disappointments and frustrations in your life.

PSP: *In some people it leads to depression and in others it seems to lead to increased ambitions.*

Rodgers: If you have the philosophy that you're going to enjoy life, and do the best you possibly can—it's going to pay off for you in the long run.

PSP: *What is the core of your belief system, if you had to sum it up in one basic principle?*

Rodgers: The thing I stress all the time is that you have to do a thousand things 1 percent better, not just do one thing 1,000 percent better. It's doing the little things well, being on time for meetings, returning phone calls, saying "thank you" to people. It sounds like a simplistic cliche, but that is the reason one organization or one person is successful and another is not. The secret is that everybody knows what they ought to be doing, but the ones who practice daily excellence are the real "difference makers."

PSP: *It sounds like a game of inches—like a constant victory over yourself.*

Rodgers: That's true. And that's why I find the line between success and failure, whether it's personal or business, so thin that you often don't know what side of the line you're on. With a little extra effort and a positive attitude, the problem goes away. But some people never seem to understand that point.

12

One Minute Selling
Dr. Spencer Johnson

"Sales people who work in the present do better work. They don't divide their energy with worry over the next sale, or yesterday's missed opportunity. When all your energy is focussed on the here and now, you're more productive."

Successes can be achieved minute by minute, according to Dr. Spencer Johnson, who became a subject for this interview when his book *The One Minute Salesperson* (coauthored with Larry Wilson, New York: William Morrow & Co., 1984) hit the stands. Johnson is well known for his "one minute" philosophy, but few people realize how many hours, weeks, months, and even years go into his seemingly simple presentation.

If it is true that the easier something appears on the outside, the more work has gone into putting it together, then we can assume that Johnson's one minute success streak had its roots in years of research and experience. An avid believer in living in the present, Spencer Johnson, a medical doctor by training, practices what he writes, speaks, and preaches. His decision to become a teacher of health rather than a healer of sickness indicates just how far he had to travel away from his initial commitment to medicine.

Johnson now looks upon most illnesses as self-imposed, or at least self-perpetuating. While working in hospitals, Johnson saw hundreds of patients who viewed themselves as victims. They believed nothing could be done for them and they felt doomed. Those who could accurately assess their own feelings, who took an assertive posture toward their own possibilities for change and growth, no matter what the limitations outside, were the ones who were most likely to become well again. At the very least they could function successfully within the constraints that were presented.

For those patients who chose to remain victims of circumstances, there was little hope for positive change. Dr. Johnson has explored many different techniques for overcoming self-defeating attitudes. For example, the person who plays the game, "I'll be happy when . . .," is doomed to remaining unfulfilled in his search for happiness. The person who tells him- or herself that happiness is a state that exists right now is more likely to experience that happiness.

Putting conditions on one's feelings results in poor performance and poor feelings. Setting up conditional happiness, success, or other outcomes leads to ever-increasing feelings of frustration. But setting up dual happiness, happiness for both now and later, allows for good moments at any time.

Johnson's technique of living in the present doesn't allow negative attitudes to fester. A setback is only one moment in time. It ends. The next moment is up to you, says Johnson. Make that next moment one of learning and the growth will happen by and of itself. Before you know it, you will be where you wanted to be from the start.

Spencer Johnson has been an inspiration to millions of us to live now, to be happy with who we are now, and to allow ourselves to grow in the future. There is no justification, in Johnson's view, for hanging on to old wounds and miseries. Johnson himself has had his share of hard knocks. He even mentioned, in passing, the pain of failed relationships. But he would not allow himself to dwell on those past failures—to live as if they were still alive.

His lesson is subtle. His words seem glib. Hidden within the message is a pioneering effort to lift the collective spirit and to let it fly free.

"You are not your sales. You are the person behind your sales," says Spencer Johnson, M.D., coauthor of the record-breaking best seller The One Minute Manager *(New York: William Morrow & Co., 1982), and author of the best-selling book,* The Precious Present *(New York: Doubleday, 1984). The prolific and multi-talented Dr. Johnson, along with Larry Wilson, has just coauthored* The One Minute Salesperson: The Quickest Way to More Sales with Less Stress. *In this exclusive interview with* Personal Selling Power, *Dr. Johnson shares valuable insights about work, goals, selling, and success.*

"It took me 40 years to learn that I don't have to get any better. I can have a gift simply by enjoying the present." This sage advice comes from a true winner.

PSP: *How do you explain the phenomenal success of your book, The One Minute Manager?*
Johnson: Most people are overwhelmed by the amount of

information in this over-communicative society. *The One Minute Manager* became so successful because it tells people something very simple—something that works!

PSP: *What is that?*

Johnson: Well, it tells them how to manage in a simple way that they can use immediately. Also, the timing was good because business people were looking for good management techniques.

PSP: *Do you see a connection between the popularity of computers and the popularity of your ideas?*

Johnson: It's interesting to me that when I wrote my last two books using a computer, I thought that it would be a distracting tool. But I found that the computer helps me to think clearly and logically. It's so fast and compatible with the way the mind works. And that leads to the idea that the more sophisticated our world becomes, the more the need exists for people to be touched.

PSP: *Are you talking about metaphorical touching?*

Johnson: No, I'm talking about the need people have to feel cared about—to feel that they somehow make a difference. People get upset and don't perform very well when they feel that they are living in an impersonal world—when they feel that they don't really make much of a difference.

PSP: *What would you call this phenomenon?*

Johnson: Generally this is known as the need for high touch. As the world becomes ever more complex and we are asked to deal with complex issues, we have to find simpler ways of managing those complexities.

PSP: *How did you make the complex transition from physician to author and motivator?*

Johnson: Working with patients in a hospital, I always saw bad attitudes. I became convinced that bad attitudes can create illness. I realized that if you could make yourself ill, you could make yourself well. And I thought, "Why am I going to spend 50 years helping people after they've gotten sick? Why not help them to see that they can do things with their minds to keep themselves well?"

PSP: *What did you perceive was making them sick?*

Johnson: These hospital patients had one thing in common. They all viewed themselves as victims—as under the control of something outside of themselves.

PSP: *In a world that often victimizes people, how can you not view yourself as a victim?*

Johnson: As long as you view yourself that way, you can't. If you think the world victimizes you, you're in trouble. The reality is that nobody cares one way or the other about you. So they are not really victimizing you. But if you view it that way, then that gives them power over you. If you can learn to view the world in positive, upbeat terms, then even when bad things seem to be happening to you, you can realize that it's only for a limited time. The question then is do you go down or not?

PSP: *Would you agree with Zig Ziglar's statement that you'd better be tough with yourself or the world will be tough on you?*

Johnson: I would agree with that if he would insert the word "behavior." It's good to be tough on your behavior but it's very unwise to be tough on yourself. In *The One Minute Salesperson* Larry Wilson and I talk about praising yourself within the context of a self-management system. Praising yourself for doing something right can be a strong antidote to self-talk that is overly tough.

PSP: *Does anyone have the power to tell you whether you're O.K. or not?*

Johnson: No one has the power to say whether I'm O.K. or not. I alone have that power. The point is—we're all O.K.

PSP: *So, that's a given. . . .*

Johnson: Absolutely—that's not up for grabs. Even if you fall below your sales quota, that's not who you are. You are not your sales. You are the person behind your sales. . . .

PSP: *Your newest best-selling book is called* The Precious Present. *How does the title relate to salespeople?*

Johnson: I suspect that I'm like a lot of salespeople in that they don't need to get any better than they are right now. They don't need to learn anything. They can have a gift simply by enjoying the present.

PSP: *I thought of my 4-year-old daughter all through your book.*

Johnson: Well, that's a very good point. We all knew how to enjoy the present at some time. But most of us have forgotten it. Salespeople who work in the present do better work. They don't divide their energy with worry over the next sale, or yesterday's missed opportunity. When all your energy is focussed on the here and now, you're more productive.

PSP: *What did you anticipate the reception of this book would be?*

Johnson: It never occurred to me that business executives and sales managers would buy *The Precious Present*. I saw it as a general book. But now I see that business executives need to be reminded not to carry each successive problem around all day long. You can solve a problem and move on and forget the past one.

PSP: *Have you achieved all your goals?*

Johnson: I hope not.

PSP: *Are goals important?*

Johnson: Well, I fell into the trap of "I'm going to be happy when . . ." I set all kinds of goals and then expected that upon reaching one, the next one would make me happy. I remember playing tennis and looking up at the hill beyond the club and thinking, "I'd love to have a house on the hill." I played lousy tennis and I delayed getting the house on the hill.

PSP: *Did you ever get your house on the hill?*

Johnson: Yes, I did, but not until I started to appreciate what I had and didn't compare it to what I thought I wanted. It wasn't until I started to live in "the precious present" that I became the most productive and profitable.

PSP: *How did you sell your first book to a publisher?*

Johnson: [Chuckles.] That's where I learned my first lesson in sales and marketing. I had a manuscript called *Fraternity Row* and I sent it around to all kinds of publishers in New York and I just couldn't make a sale. So I decided to package it, which was a new idea to me. And finally I realized that everyone loves a winner, so I packaged it as if it was already a winner. I went to a well-known actor named Dick Powell and asked him to write a foreword for my book.

PSP: *How did you know him?*

Johnson: I didn't—I just knocked on his door at the studio where he worked.

PSP: *And he let you in?*

Johnson: No, he told me to go away.

PSP: *What did you do then?*

Johnson: I told him, "Look, I don't want to get into motion pictures. I don't want a job." So he said, "In that case come on in."

PSP: *That's a terrific cold-call technique.*

Johnson: I told him I was a fraternity brother, and sure enough he read the book, liked it, and wrote the foreword. Then I sent his foreword to 13 other very famous people and asked them if they would comment on what they thought of college fraternities. And they did.

PSP: *How can salespeople approach the problem of the overloaded prospect who just doesn't want to look at one more product?*

Johnson: Well, first that salesperson has to be sold on him- or herself. Then you must think of the other person. What are you bringing to him that will interest him? People don't care what's important to you, they care what's important to them.

PSP: *What do you have to know to be good in sales?*

Johnson: There are certain techniques that the outstanding salesperson seems to use automatically, like visualization and projection. And of course timing and a good sense of when to close and when to stand back. One of the best ways to realize how good you are is to catch yourself doing something right.

PSP: *What is your measure of success?*

Johnson: My measure of success is how peaceful you are with yourself regardless of what's going on around you. But my measure used to revolve around goals. I would set a goal and go after it. If I got the goal, I felt I was a success. If I didn't get the goal, I felt frustrated. The problem with making your happiness dependent on a goal is that when you achieve that goal, you're bound to say, "Is that all there is?"

PSP: *What about happiness?*

Johnson: Happiness is right now. If you're not happy right now, you're never going to be happy. If you can't be happy right now, even if things don't look too good, you're never going to be able to make things just the way you want them. That's the great message in *The Precious Present.*

PSP: *What is the advantage of living in the present?*

Johnson: Once you start savoring and accepting what you are and what is happening in the present, you get enormous personal power and energy. This is particularly true in sales. Salespeople who are not together themselves make customers anxious and defensive. They won't let those salespeople in and they won't buy from them either.

PSP: *Do you see a division between past, present, and future?*

Johnson: No, there is none. There is only the present. Life is a series of present moments.

PSP: *What is the present like for a salesperson who has just lost a sale?*

Johnson: He's probably down. He's *not* living in the present. He's very into what he thinks it ought to be. He can't change anything about that sale. He can't go back and grab the prospect by the throat. But he can say to himself, "Right now is a very good moment in my life. And there's a purpose but I just don't know what it is yet. I will learn something from this." If you see each selling experience as part of a continuum, it will energize you. If you don't see it that way, you get demoralized. And you go into your next sales call down.

PSP: *Why don't we live in the present?*

Johnson: Most of us were not trained to live in the present. We were trained to get ready.

PSP: *Do you ever procrastinate?*

Johnson: I'm doing it right now. I don't always live in the present. I don't always do what I know. I don't think any of us do. But the more often I do it the better my life works. Procrastination is the worry about the future.

PSP: *How can salespeople reconcile their need for the immediate gratification of a sale and the management part of selling, like follow-up and paperwork?*

Johnson: Everybody has a problem with that. I constantly get asked, "What about planning for the future?" My answer to that is to be in that moment. Even if that moment is paperwork or planning. Then you won't be living in the future. Realize that paperwork is part of selling. If you view a sale as only that fraction of a second when the customer says yes then you're going to view everything else as a waste of time.

PSP: *In other words, there's more to love than just sex.*

Johnson: Exactly. You'll miss some very enjoyable moments if you view it that way. And if you do paperwork out of resentment and boredom, guess how much you're going to learn from it. But if you reflect on what you did on each sales call as you do the paperwork connected to it—if you use your paperwork as a time to reflect on your behavior—then paperwork will become a fabulous tool, a self-learning tool.

PSP: *What does it take to do that?*

Johnson: It takes a great attitude. And winners are people with great attitudes.

PSP: *Can salespeople choose their own role models?*

Johnson: Oh, of course. Most of us don't realize how many choices we have all the time. The key is awareness—being aware of the choice you are making right now. Salespeople have some of the greatest number of choices to make, since most of the time nobody knows where they are. Their managers have a general idea where they ought to be, but salespeople are out there making choices all day long.

PSP: *Have you had role models?*

Johnson: I've had a lot of role models over the years. I like to learn from what works so I watch it and try to do the same thing. That comes back to seeing the movie in your mind—

visualization. You see it before it happens. One of my best role models is Ken Blanchard. He's the expert on the psychology of plenty.

PSP: *Recent hospital studies have shown that people who are cynical actually have shorter life spans.*

Johnson: That goes back to my early experience in medicine. The cynics spent all their time in and out of hospitals. And you can even hear that if you listen to them for a little bit of time. The cynicism actually breaks down the body. It's just fascinating how we program ourselves for what happens in our lives.

Epilog

Resolution of Disappointment

When faced with disappointment, people do one of two things: Either they seek comfort or they seek solutions. Sometimes they do both, seeking comfort first, seeking solutions later. The combination of comfort and solutions is a healthy and gratifying one on many levels. It seals the wound, allows time for healing, and prepares the ground for a new try at a more successful effort. However, there is a potential trap here.

Some people get stuck in the comfort mode. They suffer a disappointment and they seek comfort. They may have a few drinks, smoke some pot, or eat a few ice cream sundaes. Then they go on with more drinks, more pot, or more sundaes as a way of dealing with all their problems. Those people will never resolve the initial disappointment and will never be able to find solutions without professional help. (Luckily, help is abundant.)

The solution seeker—the person who, when faced with a disappointment, goes directly into the solution mode, ignoring the comfort phase, also has stepped into a trap. Such a person will work all day, not to accomplish a task so much as to avoid looking inside at his or her own feelings of disappointment and the connected feelings of rage. Rage is a powerful feeling, and there is always the fear of what it will do to us if it is allowed to surface. Therefore, the solution seeker would rather not look at it at all. The workaholic becomes unable to sense his or her own feelings and is unable to recover from disappointment. Growth is limited, and although the hours put in at work are widely applauded in business, the results will never really satisfy.

In order for disappointment to be really resolved, we need to go beyond seeking comfort or seeking solutions. Talking about a disappointment with someone intelligent and caring is a good first step. Writing down one's feelings is a second step. Talking with other people about their disappointments is a third. Reading about similar setbacks experienced by other people is a fourth possibility.

Solutions are more easily found once the initial feelings of sadness and rage are accepted as natural and inevitable for growth to take place. To map out strategies for solving a problem and growing beyond it, start with the well-accepted tools of goal setting, planning, and time management. But the most important element for growth after a disappointment is creative thinking. Look at the world as if you had never tried anything before. Think of new ways to approach the problem. Engage others in your search for a successful solution. Get ideas wherever you can and whenever you talk to a person you respect. Listen with an open mind and hear not just words but the intentions behind them.

In the 12 interviews in this book there is much wisdom. But there is one thing more—experience. Every one of the supersellers in this book has had more than his or her fair share of disappointment. (Life, after all, is rife with that singular test of true greatness.) What makes them all supersellers is their common ability to grow beyond their disappointments. We can learn from their lessons and achieve more because of them. Their path is well trod; we can follow behind, read their signposts, and know, at least in some measure, what to look out for and where to plant our own seeds.

We like to read about other people. They are our beacons in the storm. It is encouraging to know that Bo Pilgrim had hundreds of unsuccessful attempts at deboning a chicken before he got it right. It is reassuring to know that Mo Siegel lost an entire mint crop and nearly went under early in his business career. We can relate to Ron Rice's trouble with the competitors that tried to squeeze his company out of the market. Big successes are only little successes that have grown up. We all have small triumphs, and we can all scale our successes up—if we know how to handle our failures and disappointments.

In every life some disappointment will be felt. In each life, therefore, is the potential for growth. If we look at life's inevitable disappointments as opportunities for growth and further development, we will be one giant step along on the road to achievement.